1.50

THE MAJESTY OF THE DIVINE HUMILIATION

King ever glorious! King ever glorious!
The dews of death are gath'ring round Thee;
Upon the Cross Thy foes have bound Thee,
Thy strength is gone, Thy strength is gone!
Not in Thy Majesty,
Robed in Heaven's supremest splendor,
But in weakness and surrender,
Thou hangest here. Who can be like Thee?
Pilate high in Zion dwelling?
Rome with arms the world compelling?
Proud though they be!
Thou art sublime, Thou art sublime.
Far more awful in Thy weakness,
More than kingly in Thy meekness,
Thou Son of God, Thou Son of God.
Glory and honor:
Let the world divide and take them;
Crown its monarchs and unmake them;
But Thou, Thou wilt reign.
Here in abasement;
Crownless, poor, disrobed, and bleeding;
There, in glory interceding.
Thou art the King. Thou art the King!

From *The Crucifixion* by John Stainer, 1887

KING EVER GLORIOUS

THE STORY OF HOLY WEEK

By
PAUL W. STREUFERT
Pastor of Our Savior Lutheran Church
New Orleans, Louisiana

CONCORDIA PUBLISHING HOUSE
SAINT LOUIS, MISSOURI

FOREWORD

It is a privilege to write a few words introducing a volume of sermons from the pen of an honored former student of mine, whose ministry has been singularly blest wherever he has labored, and who has recently been elevated to the position of President of the Southern District of The Lutheran Church — Missouri Synod. The reader will soon become aware that the plan followed in this series of ten sermons is to present and discuss for each day of Holy Week a section of the Gospel narrative which records some significant episode in the life of the Savior pertaining to that particular day of the week. By surveying the context the author is enabled to tell the story of the whole day. The pattern naturally had to be abandoned for Wednesday, because the Gospels do not record any event for that day of Jesus' activities. This gives him an opportunity of inserting an extra sermon pertaining to Tuesday. The material for Maundy Thursday is so copious that for it three sermons are included. The last one of these three could with equal appropriateness have been assigned to Good Friday. That Easter Sunday was included nobody will find strange, because the triumphant resurrection of our divine Lord was, as it were, the Amen! of Heaven on His bitter suffering for mankind. We see, then, that the general plan of the book gives the author an opportunity of marshaling before us the events the Gospels contain beginning with Palm Sunday and ending with Easter. Thus it is a section of the life of Christ which is here presented in the garb of sermonic discourses, together with the applications and admonitions of a devout, skillful sermonizer.

The reader, I have no doubt, will agree that the Literature Board is justified in asking Rev. Streufert to make these sermons available for a larger public. His preaching is not only Scripturally sound; it is live, earnest, compelling. His utterances are marked by a kindling warmth which holds us spellbound. The language is lucid and simple; the author evidently does not belong to that self-deluded group of writers who hold that obscurity is a synonym of profundity. All this is an indication that we are here dealing with a book which not only preachers may read with profit as they meditate on texts for their Lenten sermons, but which will be appreciated by the average Christian who looks for some special material to guide him in his devotions during the season of Lent.

The chief excellence of these sermons is, of course, that they portray to us, in His humiliation and His exaltation, in His beauty and majesty, Jesus as the divine Redeemer, who loved us and gave Himself for us. What else one may say in praise of these discourses, they keep before us constantly the image of Christ as the sin-bearer, the Lamb of God, our Substitute, ordained for our salvation from all eternity.

May these messages not only find many readers, but may the heavenly light and healing which they dispense vivify and cheer human hearts in every place were the book is perused.

WILLIAM F. ARNDT

PREFACE

These ten messages from the King were prepared during the Lententide of 1954 for a small group of the King's loyal subjects. Upon request they are now being offered to the brethren in the royal household of the King. Combined in the present volume in chronological order, these sermons form *The Story of Holy Week*.

The words which we have borrowed from any writer, either sacred or secular, are given in italics.

May Jesus remain the *King ever Glorious* in the hearts of men as we proclaim His story and His glory!

THE AUTHOR

CONTENTS

I	THE GLORY OF HIS PERSON	1
II	THE GLORY OF HIS PURITY	13
III	THE GLORY OF HIS PRECEPTS	23
IV	THE GLORY OF HIS PROPHECIES	34
V	THE GLORY OF HIS PASSOVER	44
VI	THE GLORY OF HIS PRAYER	56
VII	THE GLORY OF HIS PRIESTHOOD	67
VIII	THE GLORY OF HIS PASSION	78
IX	THE GLORY OF HIS PROMISES	89
X	THE GLORY OF HIS PEACE	97

I. THE GLORY OF HIS PERSON

*And it came to pass, when He was come nigh to Beth-
phage and Bethany, at the mount called the Mount of
Olives, He sent two of His disciples, saying: Go ye into
the village over against you; in the which at your enter-
ing ye shall find a colt tied, whereon yet never man sat;
loose him, and bring him hither. And if any man ask
you: Why do ye loose him? thus shall ye say unto him:
Because the Lord hath need of him. And they that were
sent went their way, and found even as He had said
unto them. And as they were loosing the colt, the owners
thereof said unto them: Why loose ye the colt? And they
said: The Lord hath need of him. And they brought
him to Jesus; and they cast their garments upon the colt,
and they set Jesus thereon. And as He went, they spread
their clothes in the way. And when He was come nigh,
even now at the descent of the Mount of Olives, the
whole multitude of the disciples began to rejoice and
praise God with a loud voice for all the mighty works
that they had seen; saying: Blessed be the King that
cometh in the name of the Lord; peace in heaven, and
glory in the highest! And some of the Pharisees from
among the multitude said unto Him: Master, rebuke Thy
disciples. And He answered and said unto them: I tell
you that, if these should hold their peace, the stones
would immediately cry out.* — Luke 19:29-40.*

A quarter of a century ago Lord Carnarvon and Howard C. Carter, after months of hard labor, finally reached the sealed doorway to the tomb of Pharaoh Tutankhamen, King of Egypt. Carter was the first to peer through the opening. He stood transfixed and speechless, not because he beheld an example of the supreme splendor of antiquity, but, as he says: *We felt that we were in the presence of the dead king and must do him reverence.* Those in the party who later entered the tomb came out stricken with awe, and for a long time could not utter a word. The glories of antiquity had cast their silencing spell about them, 'tis true, but much more so the recognition that they were the first to stand in the presence of the king, now dead these long thirty-three hundred years.

How dare we speak today, on this holy occasion, knowing that we are standing in the presence of the King ever Glorious? Would reverence not demand of us a hallowed silence? If men are silent in the presence of a king who is dead, who of us would dare to speak in the presence of the King who lives forever? But speak we must, for the King bids us speak. *We cannot but speak the things which we have seen and heard,*[1] of Him, King Jesus.

With today's service we step over the threshold into the holiest week of the year. Through the centuries this week has been considered holy by Christian people, not because men have made it holy by deeds or by abstinences, but because in this week the holiest life that was ever lived on earth reached its climax. This week will be Holy Week to us, not only because it is the week in which the Son of God died, but because it is the week in which the King ever Glorious held His triumph.

2

We have set ourselves the task of becoming better acquainted with this King and the events in His life as they happened day by day twenty centuries ago. Each day we will gather in our chapel to stand before the King. He will speak to us from His holy Word. The message He would bring us on this Palm Sunday concerns

THE GLORY OF HIS PERSON

Bruce Barton wrote a book about Jesus, titled *The Man Nobody Knows*. Norman Langford wrote a book, *The King Nobody Wanted*. Perhaps both men were right. But not altogether. Is the person of that Man so shrouded in mystery that He must remain forever within the clouds of fantasy? Is the person of that King so unapproachable that none might know Him and thus want Him?

WHO IS THIS KING?

We are not the first to have asked this question. *Who is this King of glory?* [2] David asked it long ago. But David knew. He had seen Him in his prophetic vision. It was the Messiah, *the Lord strong and mighty, the Lord mighty in battle.* [3] Therefore, *lift up your heads, O ye gates,* [4] the King is coming! When He came, Wise Men looked for Him. *Where is He . . . King of the Jews?* [5] The Wise Men learned the answer. They knew.

Thirty years later there were others. Waiting patiently for the advent of Messiah, humble men found Him by following. *Thou art the King of Israel,* [6] rejoices Nathaniel after his experience at the fig tree. Nathaniel knew. Three years later the multitude of rejoicing disciples cried out, as He came down the Mount of Olives

3

on that first Palm Sunday, *Blessed be the King!* They also knew.

Do you know Him? Look at Him more closely in this Palm Sunday story. It is quite possible that some among us today have never heard this story. The boys and girls seated before our altar, who will renew their vow of faithfulness to the King this morning, know the story well. It is a simple story which tells us much about the person of the King.

Our Savior had completed the work that His Father had sent Him to do. The time of teaching and preaching and living His holy life as a substitute for all the world was drawing to a close. The time was drawing near when the King must also lay down His life for His subjects. The days were at hand which filled the King Himself with trembling. Those days of Holy Week would shake to the deepest foundations the faith of men. Men who said they were strong would become weak. Men who said they were certain would become doubters. Men who said they would fight valiantly would run from the battle. Men who had been called to lead would turn traitor.

The King knew His throne would be a cross. *He went before, ascending up to Jerusalem.*[7] On His last journey to the Holy City His disciples are with Him. As they come close to the villages of Bethphage and Bethany, Jesus singles out two of the disciples and says quietly to them: I should like you to walk ahead into the village that lies over against us. Near the entrance to the village you'll find a place where a colt is tied. No one ever sat on that colt. I want you to take the colt, untie it, and bring it to Me. If anybody tries to stop

4

you, all you will have to say is, The Lord needs the colt, and he will let you have it.

And so the two disciples rush off into the village. There's the colt, tied just as Jesus had said. They walk up to it, untie the rope, and, lo, there are the owners of the colt. What do you want with the colt? The disciples have their answer ready: The Lord needs him. Without dispute the owners permit the two to walk away with the colt.

Who is this King who can look into a distant village and see a lowly animal tied? Who is He that can so direct the hearts of men that without dispute they permit their beast of burden to become His royal carriage? He must be more than Galilean carpenter. He must be more than teacher. Yea, He must be more than man! He is more!

The King Is God

This King ever Glorious demonstrated in all the days of His earthly ministry that He is God. He wore no crown, and yet He commanded the wind and the waves to be still. They obeyed. He wore no crown, and yet He brought the fish of the deep into the nets of the disciples in great drafts of fish. They obeyed. He wore no crown, and yet leprosy and palsy and lameness and blindness and deafness and the devils themselves had to flee before Him. They obeyed. He wore no crown, and yet the very doors of death had to fly open and give back the living in Nain and Bethany and Capernaum at the command of the King. Who can command such obedience but God? This King is God.

The Hebrew Prophets knew that this King would come. They all had predicted the glory of His person.

5

Isaiah said it. *His name shall be called . . . The mighty God.*[8] Jeremiah said it. Holding up the Messiah, the lowly Nazarene, to the gaze of the world, he shouts, *Behold, the days come, saith the Lord, that I will raise unto David a righteous Branch, and a King shall reign.*[9] Daniel said it. Beholding the King with prophetic eye, he says, *There was given Him a kingdom which shall not pass away.*[10]

But more. When speaking about this King and His person, the holy Bible from Genesis to Revelation gives Him names that belong only to God, characteristics that belong only to God, abilities that belong only to God, and honor that belongs only to God. *In Him dwelleth all the fullness of the Godhead bodily.*[11] Therefore these boys and girls, who in a few moments will swear eternal allegiance to the King, have learned to say in childlike faith, *I believe that Jesus Christ, true God, begotten of the Father from eternity, and also true man, born of the Virgin Mary, is my Lord.*[12] To them He is King, because He is God. They know. They are convinced. They are sure.

If He is what Scripture says He is and what we believe and confess Him to be, *God of God, Light of Light, Very God of Very God,*[13] then He can bring us life's greatest blessing, for

THE KING IS THE PRINCE OF PEACE

Our story continues. The disciples bring the colt to Jesus. They take their garments, put them on the colt, and then set Jesus upon them. The multitude that has now gathered begins to chant, *Hosanna to the Son of David.*[14] *Blessed be the King that cometh in the name of the Lord; peace in heaven, and glory in the highest!*

Is it not remarkable that the song of the angels at the King's birth became the Palm Sunday song of the marching multitudes? At Christmas it was *peace on earth*.[15] On Palm Sunday it was *peace in heaven*. On both days it was *glory in the highest*. Christmas and Palm Sunday belong together. Earth and heaven are again united in the bond of an eternal peace. At Christmas the King, in the form of a servant, begins His sacrificial life. On Palm Sunday He begins His march to His sacrificial death. Both were needed to bring about the salvation of man.

The multitudes did not yet know the awfulness of the plan that would bring the peace of which they were singing, but the heavens knew it and joined in the chorus of man's redemption. The men and women and children who shouted those soul-stirring Hosannas did not know that before this King had conquered He would have to march through the agonies of the hill of blood. But the King knew. Resolutely He goes forward, knowing that only in the person of the King lay the hope of the world. No peace for men until the King was dead. No forgiveness for men until the King had taken all the sins of all men of all times upon Himself and made them His own. No freedom for men from the guilt, the curse, and the rule of sin, until the King had taken into His own bosom all the shafts of divine justice leveled at His guilty subjects. This is the glory of His person. This King, who rode triumphantly into Jerusalem, carried in His body all the divine, eternal powers that made man's redemption possible. This is His glory, that though He was God, yet in love He became man, so that for man He could suffer, and shed His blood, and ride triumphantly into death. That redemption brought us peace.

7

The King is coming to His capital. Who meets Him?
His enemies. They tell Jesus to stop the singing and the
chanting of the disciples and of the multitude. In kingly
composure He replies, *If these should hold their peace,
the stones would . . . cry out.* If man can be silent in
the presence of this King ever Glorious, then rocks
would give birth to heavenly harmonies in His praise.

Five days later there were others who would not
share the sentiments of the Christ about Himself. What!
This mule-riding man a king? Men of high and low
estate would not accept this as heaven's verdict. Pilate
sneers, *Art Thou the King?* [16] Mocking soldiers salute
Him, *Hail, King.* [17] Injustice asks the rabble, *Shall I* kill
your king? [18] A lost nation tolls its own death knell,
We have no king but Caesar. [19]

His enemies are determined to make His glorious
person inglorious. With spite and spit they will degrade
Him. With mocking scepter and murderous scourge they
will debase Him. With crown and cross they will defile
Him. They'll make sure He can't be king. The condemned King ascends His throne of blood. There's no
mistake in the superscription, INRI, *THIS IS THE
KING.* [20] The milling mob at the King's feet refuses to
accept the judicial taunt. The wounded King is wounded
more, *If He be King — let Him come down.* [21] He did
come down — dead!

But that is not the end of the story of the King.
Three days later, and the King is back. His resurrection
proclaims Him King. The weeping Magdalene runs from
the garden to tell the world *that she had seen the Lord,* [22]
the King. Weak men, doubting men, cowardly men,

behold the living King. They, too, run to the ends of the earth to tell His story and tell of His glory. They *turned the world upside down — saying that there is another king, one Jesus.*[23] No fire, no sword, no persecution, no manifestation of the hatred of His enemies could stop the onward march of the King ever Glorious.

The last chapter about Him has not yet been written. The King is coming back. Then men will see the glory of His person. But before Me comes, He keeps marching on in triumph through New Orleans, through Louisiana, through the South and the North, through all our country, through all the world. Wherever the Word of God is preached, there the King rides on in His triumphant conquest. *My Word shall not return unto Me void.*[24]

HIS TRIUMPH IN HUMAN HEARTS

This Jesus is most glorious when He holds His entrance into human hearts. When He came to Jerusalem, His own received Him not. But there were the few faithful who took Him into their hearts, who believed in Him, who dedicated their lives to Him. Though His person was clothed in the lowly garments of His humiliation, these simple folk saw with the eyes of faith His majesty. They *beheld His glory, the glory as of the Only-begotten of the Father.*[25]

On Judgment Day that scene will repeat itself. It will again be the few who will walk with Him into the halls of heaven. It will be only the remnant of the people who will share His triumph there, because He triumphed in their hearts here on earth. The road that leads to that eternal triumph is narrow and crooked and hard to travel, *and few there be that find it.*[26] But the road that

9

leads to destruction is wide and smooth and easy to travel, *and many there be which go in thereat.*[27]

Which road will you boys and girls in our confirmation class travel? Which door will you take into eternity? Today you make a great decision. Let me once more lay close to your heart the King ever Glorious. My sorrow as your pastor at the close of another course of instruction is that you had to depend so much on my halting words and phrases to see the King in the glory of His person. My prayer today is that I may have taught you to depend on no man's word about the King, but that you let the King speak to you Himself through the holy Bible all the days of your life. Read the Book, study the Book, love the Book, for it is to you a personal message from your King. Learn to love Him more and more who has given you that Book.

What has this Jesus ever done for you children? The first thing He did was that He brought you into this world. It was His will. Before you were born, the Savior thought of you. He saw to it that through Christian parents you were brought to the Sacrament of Holy Baptism. In that moment the King ever Glorious came into your heart. Even as a little babe, although you remember it not, you knew Him, you believed in Him, for the Scripture says, *As many of you as have been baptized into Christ have put on Christ.*[28] The King and you were then already united. His person, glorious as it was, was united with your inglorious person. You the sinner were accepted as the son and daughter of the Savior-King.

While you were little tots, your parents taught you to fold your hands and to speak to Jesus in your short baby prayers. As you grew older, your parents wanted

10

help. They brought you to Sunday school to learn more about your King. Year by year your understanding of Him unfolded more and more through instruction in school and confirmation class.

And now, have you not finished with all this business of learning? Children, confirmation is not graduation. This is only the beginning. I have given you but a tool and a weapon. Now comes the time for you to work with this tool and weapon placed into your hand by the King. It is His, not mine. Use it faithfully to build a holy castle in your heart for the King. Use it faithfully to beat down all the enemies who will attack the fortress of your heart. Your enemies are many, and they are powerful. Stay close to your King. With Him you cannot fail. With Him in your heart there will come the daily triumphs in your battle between right and wrong.

On Easter Sunday you children, robed in white, will again step to this altar to be united with the glorious person of the King. He invites you for the first time in your young lives to taste His Holy Supper. In simple bread and wine you will eat His holy body and drink His precious blood. None but the children of His royal household may partake of this holy food. You are His royal priesthood, because He has already triumphed in your hearts. Come often to the Lord's Table. Here He opens up the storehouse of His rich treasures, the treasure of forgiveness for all your sins, the treasure of peace with God your Father, the treasure of comfort in every affliction, the treasure of strength for every battle. That these treasures may be yours in fullest measure has been the constant concern of your congregation and of your pastor. Your parents and sponsors and friends have often prayed that the King ever Glorious may triumph in your life and that you by His grace and power might never fail Him.

Children, the Lord does not need you, and He does not need me. But if you and I fail Him, *the stones* under our feet will *cry out*. If your and my life will not be the triumph of the Christ in us, then the King will look to the soil, and He will raise up a new generation, from among a different people, perhaps of different color or language, who shall carry forward the banners of the King ever Glorious.

God grant that we may ever remain faithful, that the world may ever see the glory of His person through us. God, give us strength to say, *Ride on, ride on, in majesty!* [29] King ever Glorious, we follow in Thy train.

Amen

II. THE GLORY OF HIS PURITY

And Jesus went into the Temple of God, and cast out all them that sold and bought in the Temple, and overthrew the tables of the moneychangers, and the seats of them that sold doves, and said unto them, It is written, My house shall be called the house of prayer; but ye have made it a den of thieves. And the blind and the lame came to Him in the Temple; and He healed them. And when the chief priests and scribes saw the wonderful things that He did, and the children crying in the Temple and saying, Hosanna to the Son of David! they were sore displeased, and said unto Him, Hearest Thou what these say? And Jesus saith unto them, Yea; have ye never read, Out of the mouth of babes and sucklings Thou hast perfected praise? And He left them, and went out of the city into Bethany; and He lodged there. Now, in the morning, as He returned into the city, He hungered. And when He saw a fig tree in the way, He came to it, and found nothing thereon but leaves only, and said unto it, Let no fruit grow on thee henceforward forever. And presently the fig tree withered away! And when the disciples saw it, they marveled, saying, How soon is the fig tree withered away! Jesus answered and said unto them, Verily I say unto you, If ye have faith, and doubt not, ye shall not only do this which is done to the fig tree, but also if ye shall say unto this moun-

*tain, Be thou removed, and be thou cast into the sea,
it shall be done. And all things, whatsoever ye shall
ask in prayer, believing, ye shall receive.*

Matthew 21:12-22

Without doubt our Lord Jesus is the most controversial
figure in history. He will remain such until the end of
time. *The kings of the earth set themselves, and the
rulers take counsel together, against the Lord, and
against His Anointed.*[1] When the King ever Glorious
was born, King Herod sought to take His life. When
in the days of His ministry He had raised Lazarus from
the dead, the rulers *from that day forth . . . took counsel
together for to put Him to death.*[2] When in the days
of His resurrection glory the King was reborn in the
hearts of men through the spread of the Gospel, then
was fulfilled the word of the King that *whosoever killeth
you will think that he doeth God service.*[3]

While the last page of world's history is being written
and the skies become bright with the light of His second
coming, the fires of hate will still be burning on earth.
Hate and persecution of Christ's people is rooted in
hate toward the King. Hate toward the King is rooted
in ignorance, ignorance of His glory. *These things will
they do unto you because they have not known the
Father, nor Me.*[4]

What causes men to hate the Savior? The cause lies
in His spotless holiness. His blameless life is an indict-
ment of the evil in the lives of men. His purity is God's
testimony of what God required men to be. *Men loved
darkness rather than light, because their deeds were
evil.*[5] We behold the purity of the King ever Glorious

14

as we follow Him in the events of Monday of the first Holy Week long ago. May God's Spirit enlighten us with His Gospel, as we consider

THE GLORY OF HIS PURITY

Three incidents of this day are especially noteworthy. They shall guide us in our meditation and shall convince us that the unknown author of the hymn *Beautiful Savior* was not in error when he wrote, *Jesus shines brighter, Jesus shines purer, than all the angels in the sky.*[6]

> I. The Barren Fig Tree
>
> II. The Cleansing of the Temple
>
> III. The Blind and the Lame are Healed

I. THE BARREN FIG TREE

Palm Sunday had been a glorious day for the Savior. He had entered the city of Jerusalem in a triumphal procession, in which the multitudes had acclaimed Him King. With palm branches and hosannas the people had demonstrated their love for Him. By what right do we so often identify the people who sang *Blessed be the King,*[7] with the multitude which five days later shouted, *Crucify Him!?* [8] Luke calls the former *the whole multitude of the disciples.*[9] Surely they were not the ones who demanded His death!

When Christ came to the Temple, it was a different story. *All the city was moved, saying, Who is this?*[10] Here in the Temple He found those who were ignorant of His person and work, those who hated Him and plotted His death, those who had desecrated the Temple of God by their unholy traffic. Here He saw misery and woe, both spiritual and physical. With a heavy heart He returns that evening to Bethany for rest and quiet. Oh, holy night, enfold Him in thy silent mantle of sleep, and let Him come forth strong, for there is *a sound of battle in the land. . . . The Lord hath opened His armory, and hath brought forth the weapons of His indignation*,[11] and they shall strike the King.

Could He sleep that night, knowing the spiritual condition of His people and the hatred of their leaders? In the morning Jesus and His companions come back to Jerusalem. He was hungry. Along the wayside He saw a fig tree. Thinking that He might refresh Himself with some fruit, He walks over to the tree, but finds nothing except leaves upon it. Suddenly the barren tree becomes to Him a picture of His own barren nation. Leaves, everywhere leaves, but no fruit. He curses the tree, *Let no fruit grow on thee henceforward forever*. The tree withered. When the disciples saw it, they were amazed. *How soon is the fig tree withered away!*

What was Jesus teaching the disciples? Here in the withered tree they saw a symbol of Israel. Jesus is not only *the Lamb of God which taketh away the sin of the world;* [12] He is also the *ax laid unto the root of the tree*,[13] He is the fan in the hand of God by which *He will thoroughly purge His floor*.[14] As the immaculate Son of God He *is a consuming fire*.[15]

ISRAEL, BARREN AND BITTER

How great the contrast between Israel and Israel's King! Israel was the seed of Abraham and so was *flesh born of flesh*.[16] But Israel's King was the Seed *made of a woman*,[17] and He was spiritual, holy, blameless, for

He was *born of the Spirit*.[18] Israel was but an earthen vessel to hold the Messianic promises, but the King was the Messianic fulfillment which should pour forth from that vessel. Israel was a barren tree, but the King was the *Tree of Life* [19] upon which men would find the fruits of righteousness and salvation. *This is His name whereby He shall be called, THE LORD OUR RIGHTEOUSNESS.*[20]

Of the Rock that begat thee thou art unmindful, and hast forgotten God that formed thee,[21] Moses sings before his last ascent up Mount Nebo. *And that Rock was Christ,*[22] Paul replies. Not only was Israel barren, but when it bore fruit, the fruit was bitter. *Their grapes are grapes of gall, their clusters are bitter.*[23] That is Moses speaking. *He looked that it should bring forth grapes, and it brought forth wild grapes.*[24] That is Isaiah speaking. *Israel is an empty vine.*[25] That is Hosea speaking. Israel, barren and bitter!

THE CONTRAST

In contrast, behold the King in the glory of His purity! *Holy is His name,*[26] sings Mary in her Magnificat, with the King in her womb. *A Light to lighten the Gentiles,*[27] chants Simeon in his Nunc Dimittis, with the King in his arms. *God anointed Jesus of Nazareth . . . who went about doing good,*[28] sings the New Testament chorus of the King's biographers. The King Himself is not unconscious of His own purity. *Which of you convinceth Me of sin?* [29] This is the challenge of Christ to the world to convict Him of any word or act that was sinful. The Apostle Peter, writing what God told him to write, puts it this way, *Who did no sin, neither was*

17

guile found in His mouth.[30] Even the devils of Capernaum have to join in the paean of praise to His purity. *Thou Jesus of Nazareth . . . I know Thee who Thou art, the Holy One of God.*[31]

THE CLASH

In the light of all this, can we marvel that *the fig tree withered away?* Can we marvel at the indignation of the King in His purity when He came face to face with the impurity of His rebellious people? The disciples had to learn that no nation could turn its back upon God with impunity, no nation could survive if it substituted its own will for God's will.

Have we learned the lesson? The people of our nation and of many other nations are deeply concerned about the clash between the ideologies of the nations in the East and our own in the West. The keen observers of our times envision a fight to the finish between *their way of life* in the East and *our way of life* in the West. Men view with fear and trembling the ultimate withering effect of such a clash. Is it not high time for us to learn the lesson, that the most disastrous clash is not between *their way* and *our way*, but between both of our ways and *His way?*

What is *our way of life?* What have we to boast of? We, like Israel, are filled with national pride. *We be Abraham's seed.*[32] For the Jew that was the ultimate. *We be Americans.* That settles the argument about the worth of anything we possess. We, like Israel, are filled with racial pride. For the Jew it was the *dirty Samaritan.* For us it is the *dirty foreigner.* To the Jew, heaven's benediction came with Jewish blood. To us, white souls come with white skins. We, like Israel, are filled with

18

greed. To the Jew it was God in one hand and the shekel in the other. To us it is a closed prayer book in one hand and the open bank book in the other. We, like Israel, are an adulterous nation. To the Jew it was merely a question of having Moses' endorsement for his *bill of divorcement*.[33] For us it is merely a question of what railroad to Reno. We, like Israel, have raised disobedient children. The Jewish youth nullified the command to honor father and mother by his simple *Corban*.[34] The American youth nullifies it with his disrespectful *So what?*

Where is boasting then? [35] — *Are we better than they? No, in no wise; for we have before proved both Jews and Gentiles,* and Americans, too, *that they are all under sin.*[36]

Here lies the clash between us and God. The withered fig tree is to us a mighty call to repentance. Let us stop comparing our life with the life of the neighbor. Our Old Adam will always find a way to draw the longer straw. Let us learn to compare our life with the purity of God's Son. Then shall we see how far we have *come short of the glory of God.*[37] In the recognition of our guilt let us fly to the feet of our King and plead for mercy. By His Gospel the Holy Spirit will open our eyes to see the glorious truth that the purity of the King was laid into the balances of God to remove the withering blast of His eternal justice. This is the glory of His purity.

II. The Cleansing of the Temple

When Jesus and His disciples came to the Temple, they saw the same traffic of yesterday. There seemed to be no end to this selling and buying in the sacred precincts, with its accompaniment of avarice and dis-

19

honesty. Pilgrims came to the Passover from all parts of the world. It was not wrong for the Temple servants to have available the necessary sacrifices which the pilgrims would need for the festival. Neither was it wrong to have a place of exchange where the people could get their half shekel *for the Temple tax in exchange for ordinary money.* But this was wrong, that the money-changers had turned a holy thing into a racket. The sellers of doves and sheep were out for profit. The buyers were as guilty as the sellers. The highest religious festival of Israel had little semblance of religion.

The King in His purity comes to His Temple and finds it impure. He throws out the religious racketeers. He overthrows the tables of money-changers and the seats of dove sellers. Isaiah supplies Him with sufficient justification for His righteous wrath, *It is written, My house shall be called the house of prayer.*[38] The priests had all their livelihood from the sacrifices brought to the Temple by the people. But they were not satisfied with this. By their cheating and stealing they had made the Temple of God *a den of thieves.*

Only the purity of the King can reform, can restore purity to the King's castle. *A king that sitteth in the throne of judgment scattereth away all evil with his eyes,*[39] said the wise Solomon. Where the King ever Glorious comes to His Temple, His purity will cleanse it. That is its glory. With His mighty *It is written* the evil is scattered, and purity again reigns.

It was so in the days of His flesh. It will ever be so when thieves and robbers gain control in His Temple. What cleansed the church in the Middle Ages of its indulgence traffic, its buying and selling of cardinals' hats, its bestowal of bishoprics to the highest bidders?

20

What cleansed the church of the pernicious influence it had on things spiritual as well as things political? No man, no Luther, no prince, no duke, no book, no writing! It was the King whom men once again saw in the glory of His purity. Once again they heard the source of all reforming power. *It is written!* Out of that advent of the King the church came forth cleansed and purified. Overthrown were the seats of those who peddled their own mental doves of doctrines. Cast out were those who had exchanged the precious truth of God for the lies of men. A clash there was, but the purity of the King prevailed.

To keep that church pure will require more than teaching teachers and preaching preachers. It will require the daily return of the King in His purity to His temple, the temple of your heart. *Know ye not that ye are the temple of God?* [40] Let us not fool ourselves. *Keep thyself pure,* [41] lies beyond our human capabilities and will power. No heart has ever been cleansed by law, either human or divine. That takes place only when *the King of glory shall come in.* [42] — *Behold, I stand at the door and knock.* [43] I am thy King. Open the door of thy heart, and I will come in with My redeeming grace, My forgiving love. Believe Me that I am thy Savior. Accept the pardon I offer thee. Know that the purity of My life and the innocence of My death made full atonement for thy impure life. This is My glory as thy King.

III. The Blind and the Lame Are Healed

Is it any wonder that they came to Him, the blind and the lame, the sick in heart and sick in body? If this King could thus cleanse the Temple, could He not

21

cleanse their bodies of the ravages of sin? They did not have to wait long for an answer. He who could cleanse the soul could also cleanse the body. They *came to Him in the Temple, and He healed them.* The body of man has been defiled by sin. Sin brought with it not only death, but sorrow and sickness. From birth to death our living is no more than a process of dying. All was the result of sin. *The day that thou eatest thereof thou shalt surely die.*[44] Man is still eating the forbidden fruit. He has pleasure in his self-inflicted wounds. *Those wounds heal ill that men do give themselves.*

Our age has been remarkable for its advance in medical science. But every new drug discovered to aid us in our combat with disease, every hospital, every clinic, every doctor's office, every wheel chair, every bottle of medicine, is a reminder of our origin and of our destiny. No drug, no serum, no physician can touch the deep-seated cause of our misery, our sin. Only He who said, *I will restore health unto thee, and I will heal thee of thy wounds,*[45] can remove both cause and effect. When our impure bodies are touched by the purity of the King, then only shall we be healed. *And the whole multitude sought to touch Him, for there went virtue out of Him, and healed them all.*[46]

Faith is the hand that reaches out to touch that power. *All things, whatsoever ye shall ask in prayer, believing, ye shall receive.* He who comes to the King in faith is healed — healed in soul by His mercy, and healed in body according to His gracious will.

This is the glory of the purity of the King ever Glorious. It bestows fruit upon the barren, it brings cleansing to unclean temples, it brings healing to sin-sick souls. Do you know your King? Amen.

III. THE GLORY OF HIS PRECEPTS

But when the Pharisees had heard that He had put the Sadducees to silence, they were gathered together. Then one of them, which was a lawyer, asked Him a question, tempting Him, and saying, Master, which is the great commandment in the law? Jesus said unto him, Thou shalt love the Lord, thy God, with all thy heart and with all thy soul and with all thy mind. This is the first and great commandment. And the second is like unto it, Thou shalt love thy neighbor as thyself. On these two commandments hang all the law and the prophets.

Matthew 22:34-40

In the days of World War II a ship crowded with refugee children from Europe was crossing the cold Atlantic. Midway in its crossing the stillness of the night was rent with the horrible sound of an exploding torpedo. The ship began to sink. As hundreds of children were plunged into the icy waters, the dark night was made hideous with their screams. Among the passengers was an American newspaper reporter. As best they could, the children and adults tried to save themselves by clinging to any piece of wreckage. The reporter noticed that one after another of the voices were silenced as the small children slipped away into the deep. Other ships finally came to the rescue. When the reporter was brought on board ship, he was asked to describe the disaster. His lips seemed to be sealed in silence. After several hours he could utter no more than the four simple words, *The darkness was horrible.*

In the spiritual world something similar is happening every day. As the dreams of men for a better world here on earth are being shattered, as their hopes for national and international security are sinking lower and lower, as the prospect of new days and new deals vanish, there is catapulted into the darkness of eternity a vast host of dying men and women. The funeral procession of the nations moves on in relentless monotony. As the German dramatist Goethe called out on his deathbed, *Mehr Licht! Mehr Licht!* so men from all walks of life cry out today, *More light! More light! The darkness is horrible!* Yes, it is horrible, but there is light. If men would only learn to come to the King ever Glorious, *the Light of the world,*[1] they would have light, not only for their dark hours of dying, but for their dark hours of living.

That you might have light in your life as well as light in your death, I invite you to sit with me at the feet of the King ever Glorious. Under the Spirit's blessing we shall profit by His instruction.

THE GLORY OF HIS PRECEPTS

I. The Events of Holy Tuesday

It is Tuesday of Holy Week. According to the sacred record this must have been the busiest day in the life of our Lord. The previous night, as so many others, had again been spent in the village of Bethany. Early in the morning Jesus and His disciples are already on the way back to Jerusalem. Along the roadside they see the fig tree which had withered because Jesus had cursed it.

A discussion develops among them about the tree. The Savior tells them that, if they had faith, they would be able to do more than He had done to the tree, they would remove mountains. *All things, whatsoever ye shall ask in prayer, believing, ye shall receive,*[2] the Lord says, drawing from the tree a lesson on prayer.

Arriving in the city, the group immediately goes to the Temple. Here He would find hundreds of people who desperately needed His instruction. Friend and foe come under the influence of His words. Hardly had He begun the instruction of His friends, when the foes were already there to interrupt with the question about the source of His authority. Since they could not answer the question Jesus gave them in rebuttal, *The baptism of John, whence was it?*[3] the Lord tells them, *Neither tell I you by what authority I do these things.*[4]

The instruction continues. On this day Jesus gave to the world no fewer than seven of His great parables, the parables of the two sons, the vineyard, the wedding garment, the ten virgins, the porter, the fig tree, and the talents.

While the King was busy with His work of construction, the Temple underground was busy with its plans of destruction. A busy day for Him, indeed, but also a busy day for them; they plotted His death. This was the day on which the Greeks pleaded, *We would see Jesus,*[5] but also the day on which Judas sold his soul, *What will ye give me, and I will deliver Him unto you?*[6]

This was the day on which the Savior clashed violently with the various religious bodies which were at enmity among themselves, but united in their hatred of the Christ. The Pharisees sought to trap Him with the question about paying taxes to Caesar. The Sadducees sought to trap Him with the question about the resurrection. One of the former group comes to Him with the question about the comparative importance of God's commandments.

As we read the record of Christ's reply to the last question, we seem to note how intent the Gospel writers are on getting into the record not only the story of His death, but also the glory of His life. They want to tell future ages, as men stand puzzled before the Crucified, what this Man stood for. They want to show men that though He was crucified, He was the world's greatest Teacher. We need not fear the theological implications of this truth. Only in a decadent church is the death of Christ preached to the exclusion of His teachings. Make no mistake about it, Christ was the world's greatest Teacher solely because He was the world's only Savior. What did He stand for? What did He teach? What is the glory of His precepts?

II. Thou Shalt Love the Lord, thy God

The lawyer who came to Jesus on this Holy Tuesday and asked the question:*Which is the great commandment in the Law?* was not an earnest searcher for truth and enlightenment. Matthew says that he came to tempt Jesus. Although Jesus, who knows all things, saw the duplicity of this lawyer, yet He gives him a straightforward answer. *Thou shalt love the Lord, thy God, with all thy heart and with all thy soul and with all thy mind. This is the first and great commandment.* Here Jesus quotes Moses. Here Jesus agrees with Moses.

Did the lawyer not know Moses? Certainly he did. He was a lawyer, especially versed in all the ancient laws. But he belonged to a school of thought which was continually debating questions about the relative importance of certain laws, the law of circumcision, the law of the Sabbath, the laws about sacrifices. Which takes precedence? They had forgotten that all divine laws are equally important. Although equal, some laws are more inclusive than others. This, too, they had forgotten. They were very much like some of our neighbors who still debate the issue whether some sins are venial and others mortal. They had forgotten that *love is the fulfilling of the Law.*[7] Through Moses God had given the world a summary of divine Law. This summary, this requirement of love, carries all other requirements of God in its bosom.

This is the glory of the precepts of Jesus, that they are not His own, but those which God already gave in the creation of man and later published through Moses. *I have given unto them the words which thou gavest Me,*[8] says the Savior. Jesus was not a new law-giver, a new Moses, come into the world. The commandment of which Jesus spoke on Maundy Thursday, *a new commandment I give unto you, that ye love one another,*[9] was definitely not new. It was a new concept of love which they needed. It was a new spirit in which they should exercise this love. In later years Paul understood this difference. He wrote, *The letter killeth, but the Spirit giveth life.*[10]

DO YOU KNOW GOD?

Do we understand it? Love toward God presupposes knowledge of God. Do you know God? The atheist says: You can't know him because he doesn't exist. Fool that he is, he stands in front of a house and says: Nobody

27

built that. God says, *Every house is builded by some man; but He that built all things is God.*[11] The agnostic says: I don't know whether God is there, and I never will know. With him it is neither Yes nor No. Has he never heard that God said, *If with all your hearts ye truly seek Me, ye shall ever surely find Me?*[12]

Yes, we can know God. God has given the world a fourfold revelation of Himself. He revealed Himself in creation, He revealed Himself in the conscience of man, He revealed Himself in the Bible, and finally He revealed Himself through His Son, Jesus Christ. From God's work of creation you can know God as omnipotent and wise. From the conscience of man, which continually testifies that man has offended God and will have to give an account to Him in eternity, you can learn that God is a just God. But neither of these two revelations can tell you who God is nor what He has done for you. Only the revelation of God in His Word and the revelation of God in His Son can reveal to you the identity of God and the grace by which He saved you.

Now, someone might say: "Pastor, you misunderstand me. Do you think I don't believe there's a God?" There's the trouble! All too many in our community think that a man is saved by merely saying, when he says: I believe there is a God. Hear what the Bible says to such a man. *Thou believest that there is one God; thou doest well; the devils also believe.*[13] That faith of the head, which merely assents to the existence of God, how far has that brought man in his quest for a happy eternity? As far as the devils. They also *believe,* but they *tremble.*

From this it is evident that we need more than mere belief in the existence of a deity. We must know who the true God is, and believe in Him. Who is He? *Hear,*

O Israel, the Lord our God is one Lord.[14] Not many, but One. This God, who called Himself Jehovah in the Old Testament, revealed Himself through Jesus Christ and the Bible as God the Father, God the Son, and God the Holy Ghost. These three are One. That is poor mathematics, but it is good theology, it is religious truth.

When Philip asked Jesus, *Lord, show us the Father,*[15] Jesus had to rebuke him with the reply: *Philip, he that hath seen Me hath seen the Father.* Thus Jesus makes it very clear: To have God and to believe in Him, we need Jesus Christ, for Jesus is God. This Jesus is the God whom we are to love with all our heart and soul and mind. Loving Him, believing in Him, worshiping Him, we love and worship and believe in the only true God. Therefore the Bible says of Him, *This is the true God and eternal life.*[16]

GOD FIRST

But more. To love God *with all your heart* means to put God first in everything. Does God come first in your thinking, in your planning? Is He your first thought at morn and your last thought at eve? Do you have Him beside you at work and play as well as in church? Before you act on any decision, do you ask what God's thoughts on your decision might be?

There is a reason why Christians put God first in their lives. *We love Him, because He first loved us,*[17] says John. Our love for God has been born only out of His love for us. The greatest demonstration of God's love for man was the sacrificing of His Son Jesus for the sins of the world. In that love He has made it possible for all men to reach heaven, not by what they do or sacrifice, but by the free grace in which He offers pardon for sin to all. The cross of Calvary is the ultimate proof and climax of God's love.

Therefore, when men accept God's love, believe that the pardon has been won for them personally, then, and then only, will they have the power and motivation to love God in return. By this power they continue to *fear, love, and trust in God;* [18] by this power they *pray, praise, and give thanks* to God; by this power they *gladly hear and learn* His Word. The glory of the precept of the King is this, that it opens our eyes to see the true God, and opens our eyes to see how far we have been removed from fulfilling our duty toward Him. And then, when by His Gospel we have seen our sins rolled back into the sea of God's forgiveness, then we have the power to say, *Through Thy precepts I get understanding. . . . Oh, how love I Thy Law!* [19] Faith becomes the great dynamo which sends the power to love God with all our heart over the lines of our life. When faith is present, then we see the great glory of the precept of the King. Without that faith in Jesus *the darkness is horrible.*

III. THOU SHALT LOVE THY NEIGHBOR AS THYSELF

There was another way, however, in which the inquiring Pharisee of our story should behold the glory of the King's precepts. After the Savior had taught him the first lesson, He immediately goes on to the second. Jesus says, *And the second is like unto it, Thou shalt love thy neighbor as thyself.*

Again Jesus quotes Moses. Again Jesus agrees with Moses. The lawyer should have remembered from his study of the Law that Moses had said, *Love ye therefore the stranger, for ye were strangers in the land of*

Egypt.[20] In the days of the Savior, love among the people of Israel was a very limited thing. It was narrow, exclusive, clannish. The lawyers had not learned the lesson of the requirements of love in a former encounter with Christ. In addition to their misconception of *love*, they had a misconception of *neighbor*. A lawyer had asked Jesus, *And who is my neighbor*, trying to *justify himself*. On that occasion Jesus tells the lawyer and those standing about the cutting parable of *The Good Samaritan*.[21] They didn't understand that all the world was their neighbor, that no human being was to be excluded from their love. They had drawn very close racial lines, within which they were willing to exercise their love. To teach them a much-needed lesson, Jesus had to hold up as an example a despised Samaritan. But they would not learn!

Have we learned the lesson? Have we seen the glory of this precept of the King? Our world, like the world of Israel, is a very cold place. There is precious little love in evidence among the nations, in communities, and among individuals. Selfishness, greed, dishonesty, brutality, inhuman slaughter, hatred of majorities against minorities and minorities against majorities — these are the order of the day. We are the most blessed nation on the earth, and yet, what have we done with our bounties? Instead of being grateful and using them to the glory of God and the welfare of our neighbor, we have not used them as avenues for the expression of Christian love. In our greed we have ever sought more. Do you realize how blessed you are? According to a chart by the King Features Syndicate it took an American carpenter exactly three minutes of his working time to earn a loaf of bread, and fifteen minutes to earn a pound of butter. At the same time it took the carpen-

31

ter in Russia one hour and eighteen minutes to earn a loaf
of bread, and ten hours and fifty-three minutes to earn
a pound of butter. These are comparisons made only
one year ago. Have God's bounties made us a nation
of loving people? Yes, lovers of self.

REVIVAL OF LOVE

How shall we bring about a revival of love in our
nation? It cannot come by legislation. It must come from
within. This was the approach of Saint John. His wonderful appeal, *Let us love one another*,[22] was based solely
on the words which follow, *for love is of God*. Love is
a creation of the Father in heaven. Love will be found
only in the hearts of those who have learned to know
God and to accept Him in faith. Love of the neighbor
is the proof that man has undergone a sanctifying change.
He has, through his love in God, turned from darkness
to light, from enmity to friendship with God and man.
This is the reason why Martin Luther began his explana-
tion of all the Commandments of God with the words:
We should fear and love God that we may [23] in all things
seek the neighbor's welfare, whoever he may be. The
glory of the precept *Love thy neighbor as thyself* can be
seen only by those who have seen the glory of the King
in His redeeming grace.

When once men have seen God in His love, then they
have the power to pass the acid test of Christianity: *Love
your enemies, bless them that curse you, do good to them
that hate you, and pray for them which despitefully use
you*.[24] Then the whole world becomes neighbor to them,
the Frenchman down in the French Quarter, the Jewish
merchant on Canal Street, the Negro living one block
over, the Roman Catholic living next door, the Baptist

32

in the apartment below us, the Greek who runs the little restaurant on the corner. All of them will become neighbor to him who has seen the love of God in Christ Jesus.

How different would the homes of our community be if the love of God would have a chance to enter! Children would see the glory of the precept to honor father and mother; husbands and wives would see the glory of the precept to remain faithful to their marriage vow, neighbors would no longer hang over the back fence spreading the choice bits of community gossip, they would see the glory of the precept to *defend* the neighbor, *speak well of him, and put the best construction on everything*.[25] Let the love of God once enter, and hatred in the home will fly out the back door. Let the love of God come in, and out goes the insane desire of men, women, and children to augment the family income by means of a two-dollar ticket on the horses. Let the love of God in Christ clean out human hearts, and we'll need no clean-up campaigns to rid our community and its police force of dishonesty and crime and vice. The glorious light of the precept *Love thy neighbor* will rise on our horizon only if we face the Cross, with all its redeeming and sanctifying power.

In that Cross alone shall we find power to love God and our fellow men. That Cross alone, with its marvelous effects on the hearts of men, gives the true glory to the precepts of the King ever Glorious. Amen.

IV. THE GLORY OF HIS PROPHECIES

Jesus saith unto them, Did ye never read in the Scriptures, The Stone which the builders rejected, the same is become the Head of the corner; this is the Lord's doing, and it is marvelous in our eyes? Therefore say I unto you, The kingdom of God shall be taken from you, and given to a nation bringing forth the fruits thereof. And whosoever shall fall on this Stone shall be broken; but on whomsoever It shall fall, it will grind him to powder.

Matthew 21:42-44

Throughout this Lententide, and especially during these days of Holy Week, we are drawing close to the King ever Glorious. We have heard some remarkable things about Him as we followed Him step for step in His holy Passion. We have reached the day called Holy Wednesday. This is the one silent day in the Passion History. There is no record of any act or word of the Savior on this day. Did He perhaps spend His few remaining hours before the dreadful battle in the seclusion of Bethany? Most likely. He needed that rest, for the next rest would not come until they laid Him into the tomb.

Since the Bible is silent about this day, let us use our devotional moments this evening to look back over the teaching career of Christ. He said some remarkable things about His own future, the future of the Jewish

34

nation, Jerusalem, and the future of the world. Our text contains an allusion to this threefold prediction of our King. Let us draw near to Him and behold Him in His glory.

THE GLORY OF HIS PROPHECIES

I. PROPHECIES CONCERNING HIMSELF

The text is a portion out of the Savior's discourses on Holy Tuesday. You recall that the religious leaders were trying desperately to find some cause for arresting Christ. While He was teaching in the Temple, they came to Him and questioned His authority. When they could not answer His questions, He told them several stories or parables. These stories had a sharp edge and cut deeply. For instance, the story about a farmer who had a well-kept vineyard. Before going on a long trip, the farmer had organized everything very well and put his hired hands in charge. When the time of harvest came, the farmer sent his servants *that they might receive the fruits of it.*[1]

But the hired hands took one of them and beat him, another they killed, and still another they stoned. The farmer sent a larger group of servants, thinking that they would be more successful. But the hired hands did the same thing to these servants. At long last the farmer sent his son to gather the fruit, saying to himself, *They will reverence my son.*[2] When those wicked men saw the son, they got together and said: There he is! Let's kill him and take his inheritance. — They caught him, cast him out, and killed him.

That was the story Jesus told. When He had finished, He asked His hearers what they thought about these hired hands? What would the farmer do with them when he got back from his long trip? The Jewish leaders replied: Why, that's simple. He will miserably destroy those wicked men and get other hired hands.

That was a bad slip on their part. Suddenly they turn red, for they began to sense that the story was about them. They and their fathers had killed the prophets, and now they were getting ready to kill the Son also. They were the ones who were going to take the Son's inheritance by violence.

Their discomfort at hearing this cutting parable is Christ's opportunity once more to predict His own death. *Did ye never read in the Scriptures, The Stone which the builders rejected, the same is become the Head of the corner?* Christ uses the same Psalm which the people had used on Palm Sunday to sing His praises, to make His prophecy of His rejection by His people.

Chief priests and elders were builders in God's temple, *they had the oversight of the Jewish church.* They cast Him out as a worthless stone. The King is to have no glory in His castle, they will see to that. This prophecy of His own death Jesus had often made before to His disciples. *The Son of Man shall be betrayed unto the chief priests . . . and they shall condemn Him to death.*[3] Not only the fact of His death, but the manner of His death He predicted. They *shall deliver Him to the Gentiles to mock, and to scourge, and to crucify Him.*[4] Three years before these events He had told Nicodemus, *As Moses lifted up the serpent in the wilderness, even so must the Son of Man be lifted up.*[5]

But more. Jesus predicted the hand that should betray Him. *For He knew who should betray Him; therefore said He, Ye are not all clean.*[6] It was no guesswork when He gave the sop to Judas at the Passover. Already

36

in the earlier days, shortly before His transfiguration, He predicted that He would rise again, as Mark relates. *And He began to teach them that the Son of Man must . . . be rejected . . . and be killed . . . and after three days rise again.*[7]

Has any man ever spoken thus about his future days? Let history produce one like Him who so minutely prophesied His tomorrows. He is more than man. He could foretell His own future because time and eternity were both in His hands. He is the King ever Glorious! He is the Prophet who is far superior to Moses and David and Isaiah and Daniel. His name *is above every name.*[8] Oh, come, behold the King in the glory of His prophecies. If the prophecies concerning Himself be true, then all His prophecies are true.

II. Prophecies Concerning the Jewish Nation

There is another prophetic allusion in our story. After Jesus had called attention to His own rejection by His people, He points out that His people and nation will be rejected of God for their unbelief. The words are these, *Therefore I say unto you, The kingdom of God shall be taken from you, and given to a nation bringing forth the fruits thereof.* This was a prophecy.

God had chosen Israel as His own people to be the bearer of His Word. The Word was given to them by men whom God had chosen. Then God gave these men the words they were to write. Look at the Book of Leviticus. Check every chapter from eleven to twenty-five, and note the first verse in each chapter. It reads like this, *And the Lord spake unto Moses, saying.*[9] This Word came not from Moses, but from God. Therefore

we Christians call it, and rightly so, *The Word of God.*
Israel had been given the Word of God, not just some
book that contained the Word of God. Their Bible was
truly the Word of God. What an honor for a nation!
But they had rejected the Word.

Furthermore, God had chosen Israel to give to the
world its only Savior, the Messiah. He should come out
of the tribe of Juda, from David's family. Not just a messiah, one of many, but the only Messiah the world would
ever have. When Messiah came and called His people
to enter His kingdom, they rejected their Messiah-King.
Through this rejection Israel would lose that which made
it great, the kingdom of God.

Christ's prophecies about the Jewish nation were very
specific, *The kingdom of God shall be taken from you.*
They had the *kingdom of God* as long as they clung to
the promises of the coming Messiah. When they lost
Him, they lost their whole religion. Israel today has no
Moses, for Moses wrote of Jesus Christ. Israel today has
no Law, for *the Law was our schoolmaster to bring us
unto Christ,*[10] as Saint Paul says. Israel today is not Abraham's seed, for *they which are of faith, the same are the
children of Abraham.*[11] Israel today has no spiritual
blessings, for Jehovah promised blessings to the nations
only in the Seed of Abraham, which Seed is Christ. *In
thee and in thy Seed shall all the families of the earth
be blessed.*[12] Thus the prophecy of Jesus about Israel
has been fulfilled in the religious sterility of the Jewish
nation. *O Israel, thou hast destroyed thyself,*[13] calls the
prophet Hosea, who saw it coming.

There is another prophecy of Jesus which must be
included here. It concerned Jerusalem and the Temple.
When later in the day on that Tuesday the disciples

called attention to the Temple, *how it was adorned with goodly stones,*[14] Jesus gave them the prediction: *As for these things which ye behold, the days will come in the which there shall not be left one stone upon another that shall not be thrown down.* He prophesies the destruction, utter destruction, of the Temple. Jerusalem shall go as the Temple goes. *When ye shall see Jerusalem compassed with armies, then know that the desolation thereof is nigh.*[15]

The King found no glory in making these predictions. Two days earlier, on Palm Sunday, He wept on the occasion of His triumphal entry when *He beheld the city.* Then already He prophesied its downfall. *Thine enemies shall cast a trench about thee . . . and shall lay thee even with the ground, and thy children within thee.*[16] All this was fulfilled A. D. 70, when Jerusalem after a three-year siege capitulated to the Roman armies under Titus. The Temple was leveled with the ground, the city completely destroyed, the treasures of the people carried away, thousands of Jews crucified on the spot, the glory of ancient Israel lying in blood and ashes. In that day was fulfilled the cry of the Jews before the judgment seat of Pilate, *His blood be on us and on our children.*[17]

How terrible the King when He comes in judgment of those who reject Him! How glorious His prophecies — glorious in spite of their awesomeness! *O earth, earth, earth, hear the word of the Lord,*[18] the voice of your King!

III. Prophecies Concerning the End of the World

Once more the voice of the King will be heard in the history of this old earth. That will be on the day on which all His prophecies concerning the end of the world will be fulfilled. In that day no one will dispute His position as King. *Then shall they see the Son of Man coming in a cloud with power and great glory.*[19] Jesus was thinking of that day of His glorious return when He said to the leaders, *Whosoever shall fall on this Stone shall be broken; but on whomsoever It shall fall, It will grind him to powder.* What a strange prophecy of our Lord!

The Stone, of course, is Jesus Himself. Whoever stumbles over Him as He lies there rejected by His people in the days of His humiliation *shall be broken.* Those who take offense at His lowliness, those who in their ignorance are outraged by His lofty claims in spite of His humble birth, they *shall be broken,* they will get hurt, they shall receive stripes. But those who reject Him with *an evil heart of unbelief,* on them the Stone will fall and grind them to powder. What a terrible judgment will be theirs!

With those words Jesus points to the great day which shall usher in the end of days. What Jesus told His enemies He also told His disciples. The former were to hear it so that their hearts would be stricken with terror. Terror might make them look for the only way of escape. The latter were to hear it so that their hearts would be filled with comfort.

That day will come. *Ye shall see the Son of Man . . . coming in the clouds of heaven.*[20] That day has been set and is known only to God, *Of that day and hour knoweth no man, no, not the angels of heaven, but My Father only.*[21] No Peter, no Paul, no Mary, no Gabriel, no Michael — not one in all the created world knows, except God only. That day will come swiftly, *Behold, I come as a thief. Blessed is he that watcheth.*[22]

40

That day will be preceded by certain signs to remind men of its coming. Jesus spent much time on the Mount of Olives explaining these signs to His disciples, for they had asked Him, *What shall be the sign of Thy coming and of the end of the world?*[23] Some of the things He mentioned to them were these: there would be wars and rumors of wars; there would be famines, pestilences, and earthquakes; there would be persecution of the Christians; there would be many false prophets and false Christs, who would be able to show great signs and miracles, by which some of God's people would be deceived; there would be a power of religious corruption, which Daniel had already described, *the abomination that maketh desolate,*[24] a terrible power that would make the church like a desert through its lies and errors. Note well! This abominable thing will be standing *in the holy place,*[25] Jesus says. That is, you will find it in the church. And finally, there will be signs in the sun, the moon, and the stars, *and the powers of the heavens shall be shaken.*[26] These will all be reminders of the glory of the King's prophecy; *Behold, I come quickly.*[27]

Think of what that day means for the enemies of the King! The graves will open, all human beings who have ever lived will rise out of the earth and sea, and, behold, there is the King! Pilate shall see Him. Oh, Pilate, look! There are your hands again; they are still stained with His blood. Now there is no water to wash those hands. Pilate, there is not even one drop of water to cool your tongue.

Herod shall see Him. Herod, it is He! And look! He is arrayed in *a gorgeous robe,*[28] but it is not the one you gave Him. Look at yourself, Herod! You have no robe to hide your foul nakedness as you stand before the King.

Annas and Caiaphas shall see Him! Look, you mighty priests! There is the rejected Stone that will now grind you to powder! Remember? You heard about that Stone long ago.

Others shall see Him. Men and women from our country and neighborhood. Clarence Darrow will open his eyes as he awakens from the lagoon of Douglas Park in Chicago, where he had his friends throw his ashes, and with terror he will behold the King whom he ridiculed, the God at whom he scoffed. Mister Darrow, in life, we knew you as a brilliant man. But there's one thing you failed to learn: the meaning of the two little words, *Too late*. Now you know them.

You and I shall see Him. O glorious day! The day of days, when we shall see the glory of the King's last prophecy, *Where I am, there shall also My servant be.*[29] He told us not to be afraid when this day would dawn. He promised that He would *send His angels with a great sound of a trumpet, and they shall gather together His elect from . . . one end of heaven to the other.*[30]

What makes us so sure that we shall be among *His elect?* Why, here it is. From eternity God saw us and chose us to be with Him. In time He brought us into this world. Sinners though we were, He brought His saving Gospel to us and assured us that His Son, the King, had lived and died in our place. By the wonderful working of His Holy Spirit in Baptism and the Word, He planted faith in Jesus into our hearts. It was He who by His grace saved us through His blood, who also sent His Spirit to make us heirs of eternal life by faith. It was His work, not ours. And then He did more. He also stayed with us all through life so that we did not fall away from Him. All the powers of hell and of earth

42

could not rob us of the joy of our faith in the forgiveness of sin. He *will perform it until the day of Jesus Christ.*[31] When Judgment Day comes, we shall be standing on the right side of the King. This is certain, because the King has promised it.

Oh, come, then, and accept this King! Believe that He is your loving Lord and merciful Redeemer. For you He is no longer the Stone that shall grind to powder. He is the Rock of Ages. You can hide yourself in Him. Let the water and the blood which flowed from His wounded side be for your sin the double cure. Let the blood cleanse you from sin's guilt and power.

As you accept Him tonight, rejoice with all true believers that the prophecies of the King never fail! This is the glory of the prophecies of the King ever Glorious!

Amen

V. THE GLORY OF HIS PASSOVER

*And the first day of unleavened bread, when they killed
the passover, His disciples said unto Him, Where wilt
Thou that we go and prepare that Thou mayest eat the
passover? And He sendeth forth two of His disciples
and saith unto them, Go ye into the city, and there shall
meet you a man bearing a pitcher of water; follow him.
And wheresoever he shall go in, say ye to the goodman
of the house, The Master saith, Where is the guest-
chamber, where I shall eat the passover with My disciples? And he will show you a large upper room
furnished and prepared; there make ready for us. And
His disciples went forth, and came into the city, and
found as He had said unto them; and they made ready
the passover. And in the evening He cometh with the
Twelve.*

*And as they did eat, Jesus took bread, and blessed, and
brake it, and gave to them, and said, Take, eat; this is
My body. And He took the cup, and when He had given
thanks, He gave it to them; and they all drank of it.
And He said unto them, This is My blood of the new
testament, which is shed for many. Verily I say unto
you, I will drink no more of the fruit of the vine until
that day that I drink it new in the kingdom of God.*

Mark 14:12-17, 22-25

For twenty centuries the children of God have followed the King ever Glorious into the Upper Room, where He makes ready to share His body and His blood with those who have accepted His redemption on the cross. Perhaps nowhere in the Passion story, outside of Mount Calvary itself, do we come as close to the heart of Jesus as we do on Maundy Thursday, when He is gathered with His disciples to celebrate the Jewish Passover. To Jesus the Passover was a glorious thing. It held a deep significance for Him. As He observes this ceremony of ancient Israel, He gives unto us His followers in the New Testament a Passover that surpasses all understanding in its blessings. Here is a Passover that shall endure until the end of time, that shall be a source of strength to Christ's people, that shall surpass by far the glory of that ancient Passover. May I assist you in your preparation for Holy Communion on this sacred day. The Holy Spirit will guide us according to the promise of the King.

THE GLORY OF HIS PASSOVER

I. THE OLD TESTAMENT PASSOVER WAS GLORIOUS

The Passover of ancient Israel was truly glorious. Do you know why? Perhaps some of the children present tonight can answer that question better than some of us adults, for they have learned to know the story of the Passover in our school and Sunday school. Some of us adults are unacquainted with it because we have only recently come into the church and, therefore, have not had the opportunity given these children. Others among us were instructed so very many years ago that we have forgotten some of the Old Testament background. I am sure you will not mind if I refresh your memory by telling the story of the origin of Israel's Passover.

You remember that many years after Jacob had moved to Egypt with his family upon the invitation of his son Joseph, a Pharaoh was ruling the country who did not know the great things Joseph had done to save the Egyptians from starvation in the days of the seven-year famine. In the course of years, Jacob's family had grown to large numbers. This Pharaoh feared these people, who had settled in a section of his country called Goshen. He tried to keep them down by making slaves out of them. He was cruel. From year to year he made them work harder and harder. The more burdens Pharaoh placed on them, the more they multiplied. He even commanded the midwives to kill the baby boys of the Hebrew women. You can well imagine how the Children of Israel cried to God to take them out of this terrible slavery.

God, who loved them, heard their prayers. He sent them the great Prophet Moses, who did many miracles to change Pharaoh's heart. Because God commanded him to do so, Moses brought many plagues upon the Egyptians: the plagues of frogs, and lice, and flies, and locusts; also a plague in which many camels, and horses, and oxen, and sheep of the Egyptians became sick and died; and then a plague of darkness which lasted three days. But nothing moved the heart of Pharaoh. He had hardened his heart against God.

Finally, God told Moses to tell the people that He would bring one more plague upon the country, which would be so terrible that, when Pharaoh saw it, he would even drive the Children of Israel out of the country. This is what God would do. At midnight He would come into the land and kill the first-born in every house, *from the first-born of Pharaoh . . . even unto the first-born of the maidservant that is behind the mill.*[1] Also the first-born of the cattle should die. Every home in Egypt would have a funeral. What a curse of God!

What God sent as a curse for Egypt was a blessing for Israel. Because it was a blessing, they would have to make special preparations. God told them to take a male lamb, not more than a year old, on the tenth day of the month and keep it until the fourteenth day. This lamb was to have no sores or wounds or broken bones; it was to be *without blemish.*[2] Every family should choose such a lamb for itself. On the fourteenth day they should kill the lamb and wipe some of the blood *on the two side posts and on the upper door post of the houses.*[3]

Then they should roast the lamb with its head and legs over a fire. At night they should eat it in haste with unleavened bread, that is, bread made out of flour and water, but not with yeast. With this they should also eat bitter herbs. They should eat all of it. If anything remained until the morning, they had to burn it with fire.

God also told them to dress properly, for they were going on a journey. They were to have a belt around their waist, shoes on their feet, and a staff in their hand. *As the Lord had commanded Moses and Aaron, so did they.*[4]

And then it happened! While they were eating this strange meal, the Lord came and punished the Egyptians as He had said. In every house and barn He killed the first-born. But when He came to the houses of the Children of Israel, He did just as He had promised: *And when I see the blood, I will pass over you.*[5] All the

47

Children of Israel stayed alive. In that night they became free from their slavery, free from wicked Pharaoh, free from their cruel taskmasters. Now they could be happy again. No more would their men be beaten with the slave whips, no more would their baby boys be killed.

How must their hearts have rejoiced when they left that dark country, where they had had so much sorrow! There must have been at least two million people who had been made free, because the Bible says there were *about six hundred thousand on foot that were men.*[6] God told them never to forget that He was the King ever Glorious who had saved them and made them free. Every year they should set aside a special time to celebrate this wonderful thing that had happened to them. Each year they should do it just as they had done it the first time. And they should explain to their children what this celebration was all about.

This is how Israel received its greatest festival, the festival of the Passover. Wasn't it wonderful how much God loved these people? Wasn't it a glorious festival to remind them of His love?

II. Jesus Celebrates the Passover

Fifteen hundred years later our Lord Jesus as a faithful Jew celebrated the Passover each year. The time was now drawing near when He should suffer and die. With a deep desire He longed to participate with His disciples in this celebration and to eat the Passover lamb. The Passover had a deep significance for Him. He knew that all the ceremonies of Israel, even this Passover, could not remove the guilt of the world, but

48

that they pointed forward to the time when another Lamb should be chosen by God whose blood would have to be sprinkled upon all the homes of the world to save them from the slavery of sin and from eternal death. He knew that He was that *Lamb of God which taketh away the sin of the world.*[7] He knew that all the Old Testament promises of a Savior could be fulfilled only in Him, because He was the Son of God, the King ever Glorious, who could win the fight with the old Pharaoh.

Sometime on Maundy Thursday the disciples came to Jesus and asked Him where He wanted them to prepare the Passover meal. He selects two of them, Peter and John, and sends them into Jerusalem with the instruction that when they come into the city, *there shall meet you a man bearing a pitcher of water; follow him.* He tells them that wherever this man stops, they should go into the house and ask the owner for the guest-chamber, where the Master is to eat the Passover with His disciples. The owner would show them a large upper room, furnished and prepared. There they should make ready all things for the celebration.

The two disciples go into town, and, lo, they see the man with the pitcher. They follow him. He goes into a house. They go in, too. They meet the owner. — Where is the room the Master is to use tonight? He takes them into the large upper room. It is furnished and ready. Who is this Jesus, who can thus with infinite detail depict the events in the hours yet unborn? Here must be One who is greater than Abraham and Moses and all the Prophets! He is greater than they. He is the King ever Glorious.

The two disciples make the necessary preparations. *And in the evening He cometh with the Twelve.* Yes,

49

Jesus with the Twelve — twelve weaklings. Who can tell the whole story of this upper room? Not even the disciples attempted it. To one who was present, John, the events of the upper room loomed large in later years. When he wrote his Gospel account, he gave us five chapters, 155 verses, about the upper room, but only sixteen chapters about all the rest of the life of Christ. Matthew gave us but ten verses, Mark nine, and Luke seventeen. But these 191 verses will never exhaust the sorrow of this room, as little as they can exhaust its glory.

Behold the King as He sits at the Passover table with His weak ambassadors. While they are eating with Him the lamb and the bread and the bitter herbs, they make His last moments with them the more bitter by casting biting words at each other. There was *a strife among them which of them should be accounted the greatest.*[8] The King washes their feet to show them the depths of love of which love is capable. Peter wants no foot-washing. Peter says No! The Lord says Yes! *If I wash thee not, thou hast no part with Me.*[9] The King describes the glory of their apostleship, by which they should bless the world with heavenly treasures, *He that receiveth whomsoever I send receiveth Me.*[10] But at the table sits one whose hand clutches a different treasure. Judas, that which *thou doest, do quickly!*[11]

In His table talk the King addresses them as little children. *Whither I go, ye cannot come. Love ye one another, as I have loved you.* Peter wants to know, *Lord, whither goest Thou?* No, Peter, *thou canst not follow Me now. . . . Wilt thou lay down thy life for My sake? . . . The cock shall not crow, till thou hast denied Me thrice.*[12] The King says, *I go and prepare a place for you.* But Thomas wants to know, *How can we know the*

50

way? Oh, Thomas, *I am the Way.*[13] Philip is unsatisfied, *Lord, show us the Father.* Oh, Philip, *have I been so long time with you, and yet hast thou not known Me?*[14] The other Judas, not Iscariot, wants to know, *Lord, how is it that Thou wilt manifest Thyself unto us and not unto the world?* Oh, Judas, *if a man love Me, he will keep My words. . . . But the Comforter . . . shall teach you all things.*[15] These men shall be the pillars of the church, ambassadors of the King?

Late into the night the instruction goes on. The King must still brief His men on His legacy of peace; on the need for steadfastness; the branch must abide in the Vine; on the work of the Holy Ghost, who as the Spirit of truth would guide them into all truth; on the hatred of the world toward the King and against them; especially on the paramount position which love must occupy in their hearts and lives — love toward Him, love toward one another, and love toward the world. The King must still tell them of the joy that would be theirs when they once realized that He had *overcome the world.*[16]

Thus the King celebrated Passover with His weak ambassadors. Because of their weakness He prays His royal and high-priestly prayer. He prays for steadfastness: *Holy Father, keep . . . those whom Thou hast given Me.*[17] He prays for unity: *that they may be one, even as We are one.*[18] He prays for success: *that the world may know that Thou hast sent Me.*[19] He prays for vision: *that they may behold My glory.*[20]

How important these moments in the upper room for the weak disciples — and for us in our weakness! Who can exhaust either the sorrow or the glory of the last Passover, the Passover that closed the book of the Old Testament forever!

III. The Greater Glory of the New Testament Passover

The New Testament era was about to open. Within the next twenty-four hours the veil in the Temple would be torn in half, exposing to the view of all people the Holy of Holies with its Ark of the Covenant and the mercy seat. As God had given ancient Israel a memorial to remember His mercy, so He would give to His spiritual Israel of the New Testament a memorial of His love.

While the Passover meal was in progress, Mark tells us that, *as they did eat, Jesus took bread, and blessed, and brake it, and gave to them, and said, Take, eat; this is My body.* A short while later *He took the cup, and when He had given thanks, He gave it to them; and they all drank of it. And He said unto them, This is my blood of the new testament, which is shed for many.*

THE GLORY OF ITS SUBSTANCE

Why this strange action of Jesus? Why give His disciples bread? They had already eaten some of it. Why the cup? The cup had already passed several times among them. Note the words *of the new testament.* Here is something new. Here is something that was not included in the Old Covenant. Here is something that even now is given birth out of God's hand of grace. Yea, the glory of this new Passover shall be that according to God's will it is a *means of grace.*

How glorious are the words of Christ in their simplicity! *Take, eat; this is My body. Take, drink, this is My blood.* If He had said: Take this bread and eat it; take this wine and drink it, and when you do this, remember Me, why, that already would have been a wonderful memorial. Any ceremony by which to remember the Savior is wonderful. But Christ said some very important words in connection with the giving of the bread and wine. Those very words give this Passover its true glory. *This is My body. This is My blood.* Again I say, how simple these words! When they ate the bread, with the bread they ate His body. When they drank the wine, with the wine they drank His blood. It was not an imaginary body or imaginary blood, but His real body and His real blood. The body that would in a few hours hang on the cross was given them to eat through the bread, or by means of that bread. The blood that would be shed on the cross was given them to drink through the wine, or by means of that wine. *Search not how this takes place, this wondrous mystery; God can accomplish vastly more than seemeth plain to thee.*[21]

How men have robbed this New Testament Passover of its glory! Some say: It is all figurative. Jesus did not say: Here, this is bread and wine. The disciples could see it was bread and wine. He did not say: Eat and drink these and think of Me. He said that, but He said vastly more; that He was giving them His body and blood to eat and drink *for the remission of sins.* He was giving them something they could not grasp with their faulty intellects. Furthermore, He did not say: Here, eat this bread, I have changed it into My flesh. Drink this wine, I have changed it into My blood. Nothing has been changed. Bread remains bread and wine remains wine. But with bread and wine Christ gives us His true body and blood.

This is what the Bible teaches about Holy Communion. This is not our invention. Saint Paul said it so very plainly: *The cup of blessing which we bless, is it*

*not the communion of the blood of Christ? The bread
which we break, is it not the communion of the body of
Christ?* [22] *Communion* means *a coming together.* There
we have it. All four things are present in this Holy
Supper of the Lord: blood comes together with the wine,
body comes together with the bread, as Paul says.
Therefore all four elements are present, and not just two,
as both the Romanists and the Reformed teach. Whoever denies this truth has no argument with us, but with
the King ever Glorious. Holy Communion is His Sacrament, not ours. It is not simply a church ceremony to
help people think of Jesus. It is the New Testament
Passover, by which the New Testament Lamb would
feed men with His body and blood. This is its glory.

THE GLORY OF ITS BENEFITS

There was a glorious purpose behind this gift of the
King to His church. It is summed up in the words *Given
and shed for you for the remission of sins.* What more
do we need in life than pardon from our God? What
is it that my soul hungers for each day that I must walk
my weary way? Is it not peace with God? Without pardon there can be no peace. My sins have separated me
from God. Nothing that men or saints or angels could
do would ever restore peace between God and me. My
King saw me, He knew my plight, and He found for
me a way of escape. *Come unto Me,* He says. Here it is.
Given and shed for you. — *Son, be of good cheer. Thy
sins be forgiven thee.* [23]

What? Shall I not believe the word of my King?
Shall I go on through life haunted by my fears? Shall
I continue to *water my couch with my tears* [24] when

54

I think of the numberless ways in which I have offended my holy God? Shall I by unbelief deny myself the heavenly benefits of pardon and peace? Oh, no! This must not be! My King speaks the truth. He does not deceive me. However long I've waited to come to this Sacrament, my King stands ready to forgive. He will take away the *filthy rags* [25] of my own righteousness and give me in their place His own *crimson blood and righteousness.* All He asks of me is that I come with a repentant heart, confessing my guilt; with a believing heart, accepting Him as My Redeemer; with a renewed heart, resolving to mend my ways and by His strength to walk His ways. This is the glory of the New Testament Passover, that it grants me pardon in my sin, strength for my faith, comfort in my sorrow, newness in my life, and hope in my death. Come, then, and meet the King in the glory of His Passover!

Are you ready to sit down with the King at His Holy Table? Amen.

VI. THE GLORY OF HIS PRAYER

And He came out and went, as He was wont, to the Mount of Olives; and His disciples also followed Him. And when He was at the place, He said unto them, Pray that ye enter not into temptation. And He was withdrawn from them about a stone's cast, and kneeled down and prayed, saying, Father, if Thou be willing, remove this cup from Me; nevertheless not My will, but Thine, be done. And there appeared an angel unto Him from heaven, strengthening Him. And being in an agony, He prayed more earnestly; and His sweat was as it were great drops of blood falling down to the ground. And when He rose up from prayer and was come to His disciples, He found them sleeping for sorrow, and said unto them, Why sleep ye? Rise and pray, lest ye enter into temptation. And while He yet spake, behold, a multitude, and he that was called Judas, one of the Twelve, went before them, and drew near unto Jesus to kiss Him. But Jesus said unto him, Judas, betrayest thou the Son of Man with a kiss? When they which were about Him saw what would follow, they said unto Him, Lord, shall we smite with the sword? — Luke 22:39-49.

Again it is Lent. New Orleans is very much aware of this season. To many an Orleanian Lent is the quiet time after the roistering of Carnival and Mardi gras. From

56

Twelfth Night to Shrove Tuesday there has been gaiety plus. And now comes Lent with its change of faces, change of habits, and change of diet. To many folks Lent is something physical, not spiritual.

Saint Peter knew nothing about Lent, nothing about its observance, but he gave to the world one of the most glorious Lenten messages of all time. *Christ also hath once suffered for sins, the Just for the unjust, that He might bring us to God.*[1]

Here is the Lenten fact. Christ suffered for sins. Not His own, for He had none. But for ours. The factual story of Lent is the story of the King ever Glorious by whom God forever settled His score with sinful man.

Here is the Lenten purpose. Sin damned, but God loved those whom He had to condemn. In love He found a Substitute. God through wicked men killed the King ever Glorious so that all mankind could be free. It was a clear case of substitution, *the Just for the unjust*, the King for His subjects.

Here is the Lenten certainty. Man could not get back to God through his own will or works. Man was powerless, spiritually dead. The King of heaven alone could raise him from death to life. The redemptive work of Christ deposited the whole lost world at the feet of God.

Lent, properly observed, will do three things for us: open our eyes to see the King ever Glorious, open our ears to perceive the purpose of His coming, and open our hearts to accept the certainty of our eternal redemption. Peter would tell us: forget the rest of Lent if you will, but remember these three great purposes. These constitute the heart of Lent.

O King ever Glorious, come unto us by Thy Spirit in this holy season, and heal our wounded lives, restore unto us the joy of Thy salvation, and make us to share in Thy triumphant glory. Amen.

That this season of prayer and meditation might leave with us more than sackcloth and ashes, we shall step into the presence of the King. As we follow Him step by step on the road He took for man's redemption, we see the diminishing light of His earthly existence finally extinguished in death. But death was merely the portal to victory. Looking back over the battlefield, every step marks Him as King, every step makes Him more glorious. To keep Him glorious in our hearts and lives shall be the intent of our Lenten meditations.

From the sacred record we would share with you in this Vesper hour

THE GLORY OF HIS PRAYER

Kings are accustomed to command, not to beg and plead and pray. Kings have sought glory in their voice of authority. We remember a certain Pharaoh. *Who is the Lord, that I should obey His voice? . . . Get you unto your burdens.*[2] We remember Nebuchadnezzar. *Is it true,* he says in his rage and fury, *O Shadrach, Meschach, and Abednego, do not ye serve my gods? . . . Who is that God that shall deliver you out of my hands?*[3] Hard voices, brutal voices, commanding voices.

How different that voice we hear coming from out the deep shadows of Olivet's garden! *Father, if Thou be willing, remove this cup.* 'Tis the cry of agony, and yet the cry of a King. What brought this King so low that He now must plead, no longer command?

58

Why Is He Here?

You know what brought the Lord Jesus to this Garden of Gethsemane. He sought strength for the last great battle to regain Paradise Lost. Within the next hour He would be in the midst of His enemies. Before another sunset the battle would be over. But the bitterness of the fight overwhelms Him — the thought of the mocking, the spitting, the beating, the thorn, the scourge, the nail, the cross.

The work of this week had already taken its toll of His human energies. From His entrance into Jerusalem on Palm Sunday until this dark night of Holy Thursday He had been teaching and preaching, bringing heaven's message to men: warning to the hardened, wisdom to the ignorant, understanding to the confused, and pardon to the penitent. Every moment of this important week in His life was filled with holy activities that were the result of His intense desire to speed the coming of the Kingdom to the hearts of men. When He needed rest and quiet, He would walk the few miles to Bethany, where in the home of Martha and Mary He would find peace. At other times He would find renewed strength in the solitude of Gethsemane.

This is the place He chooses to tap the reservoir of divine power in His hour of need. Or is there no need? Is He not God? Had not His Father twice said of Him with special significance, once at Jordan and again on Mount Hermon, *This is My Son?* [4] Had Jesus not claimed as much for Himself? And when many people of His own nation would not accept Him as such and sought to stone Him, had He not asked them, *For which of those works do ye stone Me?* [5] and then received the answer, *Because that Thou, being a man, makest Thyself God.*

God He was, 'tis true, but also true man. That is why He is here. As man He could suffer. To suffer as He did, man needs strength. To gain strength, He must pray. Prayer will help Him do what He had said, *I must work the works of Him that sent Me.*[6] His greatest work was the redemption of mankind. Redemption of man required the shedding of blood. The Covenant of Blood demanded it. *This is the blood of the testament which God hath enjoined unto you. . . . Without shedding of blood is no remission.*[7] God cannot shed His own blood. But when God in the fullness of time sends *forth His Son, made of a woman, made under the Law, to redeem them that were under the Law,*[8] then this Son can shed blood, because He is true man.

That's why He is here in the garden. God needs no Gethsemane for strength, but the God-Man, *made in the likeness of men,*[9] needs Gethsemane to gain power from on high to redeem those perishing below, under the Law. He is here because by His own choice He has become our brother.

ROYAL KNEES BENT IN PRAYER

From the Upper Room the Savior had gone down into the valley, had crossed the Kidron, and now stood at the entrance to Gethsemane. Here He leaves behind eight of His disciples. The other three, Peter, James, and John He takes with Him. Deeper into the garden they go, but even these three must be left behind, at least the distance of a stone's cast, so that He might stand alone. Kings usually stand very much alone. But This King cannot stand. The oppressive weight of the world's

guilt bends those royal knees until they touch the unhal-
lowed soil. Death was stretching out its hand to grasp
the King of creation, just as it had grasped the creature
in a garden many centuries before. The King meets His
enemy on bended knee.

FATHER

Father! The first word to rend the stillness of the
night. This does not sound like the voice of a king.
It is the pleading of a child. He is a Child, the only
Child of God who could rightfully call God His Father.
All the other sons of God had by their sin forfeited the
right thus to address God. But this Son of God had forfeited nothing. Born of a virgin by the power of the
Holy Spirit, He inherited not one of the sins of the
human family. No sin stained His life, no unholy deed
besmirched His hands, no vileness sullied His lips, no
evil thought corrupted His heart.

He could call God Father, for He had never insulted
Him, had never broken His holy laws. There was no
other to whom the Son could turn in this awful hour.
Though equal with the Father in majesty and power and
wisdom and glory, He could not lay hold on those divine
attributes to save Himself from the agonies of this hour.
This is the hour when royal majesty must give way to
humiliation's weakness. His sweat turns to blood. That
stream shall not stop flowing until God and man are
reconciled by blood upon the cross.

Father! The glory of the King's prayer is this, that
it has once more placed upon the lips of all the lost sons
of God the one name that is now, by the redeeming
blood of Christ, their holy heritage, *Our Father!* And it
is the glory of Christianity that it is the only religion

which calls God by the hallowed name of Father. No other religion has it. There is no Fatherhood of God for the sinner except through the garden gate of Gethsemane, where lies the King in sweat and blood, restoring sonship to the rebellious children of God.

REMOVE THIS CUP FROM ME

Kings have found glory in drinking from golden cups. Belshazzar was one of these. He made a great feast, and *whiles he tasted the wine, commanded to bring the golden and silver vessels which his father . . . had taken out of the Temple.* They brought the golden vessels, *and the king, and his princes, and his wives . . . drank in them. They drank wine, and praised the gods of gold.*[10] This was their glory, but the handwriting on the wall, *weighed . . . and found wanting,*[11] turned their gold to ashes, their glory to shame, and their life into death. *In that night was . . . the king . . . slain.*[12]

Here in Gethsemane lies another King. He, too, holds a cup. But this cup, if He drinks it, will turn death into life, shame into glory, and the ashes of sin into the gold of salvation. Jesus knew the contents of this cup with all its bitterness.

Ancient kings compelled the condemned to drink the cup of hemlock to expiate their crimes. Here is more than hemlock. Here is Heaven's vengeance filling the cup with expiation's bitterness, the punishment *for crimes that I had done.*[13]

Every step of the King through the hours of the night would be another draft from this cup. He shrank from drinking it, and pleaded to be spared: Remove from My cheeks the kiss of Judas. It is bitter. Remove from My ears the oath of Peter. It is bitter. Remove from My heart the loneliness when My friends forsake Me. It is bitter. Remove from Me the scorn of My church and her priests. It is bitter. Remove from Me the hate of Thine own chosen people, Israel. It is bitter. Remove the lash. It is bitter. Remove the cross. It is bitter. Remove death. It is bitter to be swallowed up by Mine own creation, to die misjudged, misinterpreted, misunderstood.

Remove this cup! The Father could not, because the Trinity would not. This cup was the plan of the Holy Trinity in which the Son of God had once concurred. To remove it would remove the self-decision of the Son to serve as sacrifice to save sinners.

This is the glory of His prayer, that it is a demonstration of His weakness. If weak, then He is man. If man, then He is my Brother and *was in all points tempted like as we are, yet without sin.*[14] If the King is my Brother, then He can take my place, then He will be capable of suffering for me, dying in my stead.

The Father did not remove the cup, but He strengthened His Son for the ordeal of drinking the cup. An angel from heaven supplies comfort and strength, the creature serves the Creator. The cup remains. It must remain or lost mankind is still lost. Thank God that it did remain, for by it our *strength is made perfect in weakness.*[15]

This is the glory of the Savior's prayer in Gethsemane, that by it all the prayers of the Father's weak and suffering children have been heard. Because God would not remove the cup of bitterness from the lips of the Savior, He could and did remove it from the lips of the Savior's people.

Though small, our congregation has many cross-bearers, who have often prayed, *Father, if Thou be willing, remove this cup!* You may be one of these. Not even I as your pastor know all the bitterness that life has poured into your cup. But in the light of Gethsemane's garden, with the King upon His knees, you have learned to face your own Gethsemane and have seen the glory of His prayer.

In Olivet's garden	Only pain in my illness?
My Savior once lay.	Only heartache each breath?
As King ever Glorious	Only tears in my weakness?
He taught me to pray:	Only sorrow in death?
O Father, remove it —	No strength in my trials?
But Thy will be done!	No hope in my fears?
If Thou wilt but help me,	I come to my Father —
My victory's won.	My cup disappears.

Not My Will, but Thine, Be Done

The prayer of the King is concluded with the words *Not My Will, but Thine, be done.* How strange these words sound, coming from the lips of the second Adam in the garden, when we remember the words of the first Adam in the garden of Eden: Not Thy will, but mine. In that first garden man had a free will. Made in the image of God, his will could match the will of God in all things. He could choose, and he did choose. Oh, sorrow of sorrows, he chose the wrong and not the right! Henceforth there would be no choice, for there would be no will that would be free. His will was now in bondage. His will was a slave of his own self-chosen death. *Ye were dead in trespasses and sins.*[16] That settles it. How can a dead man choose? The choice now belonged only to God. God did choose, and He

64

chose in love. *It is not the will of your Father . . . that one . . . should perish.*[17]

This is the will of God for which Jesus prayed in the garden that it might be done. His own will, the will upon which His human nature exerted a powerful influence, shrank back from fulfilling the will of the Father. But divine love to save man conquered the human will to escape sharing the death of man.

Thy will. Oh, the glory of these two words! On this Ash Wednesday we remind ourselves that as we pass through all the familiar Lenten scenes, the glory of the King's prayer is this, that it already points to the Easter dawn. It is the glory of His prayer that in it we already behold the victory, we already see the heavens opened to receive sinners, we see the cross in its sin-conquering power, for by it, *the Lord hath laid on Him the iniquity of us all.*[18]

His Prayer in My Life

What will this prayer mean for each of us in the days that lie ahead? This is the glory of the King's prayer, that it becomes the prayer of His loyal subjects. For those who in faith have accepted the King ever Glorious as their Savior there is now but one will to motivate every thought, word, and deed of their lives. It is the will of God. With every breath we repeat the words of the King, *Thy will, not mine!*

We know we have often failed in this. That is why we are coming to Holy Communion tonight. We realize in deepest penitence that so often it was our will, not God's, that ruled our lives. *Pride ruled my will. I walked my garish way.* God had a blueprint for my life, but I scrapped it. I made my own. I thought I knew how to shape my own destiny. I thought I knew how to find happiness and security and contentment and peace. Come hell or high water, I'll know how to make decisions that will settle the issues in the battles of life; my will, not Thine!

But now it is different. I have heard the voice of the King, I have listened to His prayer in all its glory. The paraments of royal purple on our altar and pulpit remind me that in this season I walk in the companionship of the King. Tonight at His Holy Supper I receive not only pardon for my sin, release from the guilt of my transgressions, freedom from the rule of evil in my life, but I receive the power that only divine grace could engender, the power to make the will of God my own. Now the theme song of the regenerated is more than a pretty phrase upon my lips,

> *Take my will and make it Thine,*
> *It shall be no longer mine.*[19]

On the portal of my home shall be written, *Thy will, not mine.* On the door to my office or workshop shall be inscribed in letters of gold, *Thy will, not mine.* From sickroom and playroom, from sidewalk and streetcar, from train and plane, wherever my calling may place me, the world shall hear through me the echo of the voice from the Garden, for on my heart shall be emblazoned with the torches of Gethsemane the words of my King, *Thy will, not mine.*

This is the glory of the prayer of the King ever Glorious. Amen.

66

VII. THE GLORY OF HIS PRIESTHOOD

*Now, the chief priests and elders and all the council
sought false witness against Jesus to put Him to death;
but found none, yea, though many false witnesses came,
yet found they none. At the last came two false witnesses and said, This fellow said, I am able to destroy
the Temple of God, and to build it in three days. And
the high priest arose and said unto Him, Answerest Thou
nothing? What is it which these witness against Thee?
But Jesus held His peace. And the high priest answered
and said unto Him, I adjure Thee by the living God
that Thou tell us whether Thou be the Christ, the Son
of God. Jesus saith unto him, Thou hast said; nevertheless I say unto you, Hereafter shall ye see the Son of Man
sitting on the right hand of Power, and coming in the
clouds of heaven. Then the high priest rent his clothes,
saying, He hath spoken blasphemy; what further need
have we of witnesses? Behold, now ye have heard His
blasphemy. What think ye? They answered and said,
He is guilty of death. Then did they spit in His face, and
buffeted Him; and others smote Him with the palms of
their hands, saying, Prophesy unto us, Thou Christ, Who
is he that smote Thee? — Matthew 26:59-68.*

*Follow to the judgment hall, View the Lord of Life
arraigned.*[1] We will follow the King. We beheld Him
in the Garden, praying in agony. His prayer shall never

fade from our memories. Strengthened, He goes out to meet false friend and true enemy. The kiss of Judas introduces Him to those who carried the torch for the church. The church will play an important part in the life of this King. Yea, it will play an important part in His death.

The soldiers bind Jesus and lead Him to Annas, the power behind the ecclesiastical throne of Israel, father-in-law to the high priest, Caiaphas. Annas conducts his own investigation. He wants information about the disciples and the doctrine of Jesus. — Why ask Me? Ask those who heard Me. They know. — The answers of Jesus do not satisfy the former high priest. The hand of an officer whips out and smites the King. *Why?*

Ask not, O King ever Glorious, *Why?* Thou knowest the answer. It is a higher hand that touches Thee. *It is written, I will smite the Shepherd.*[2] This is the glory of Thy priesthood, that Thou shalt be both Priest and Sacrifice, Shepherd and Sheep, led forth to the slaughter, that Thy flock may not perish.

THE GLORY OF HIS PRIESTHOOD

Our text ushers us into the immediate presence of Caiaphas. Annas had sent Jesus to him after an unsuccessful interrogation. As head of the church, Caiaphas was also the head of the supreme council of Israel, the Sanhedrin. This was *the highest ecclesiatical court of the jews, composed of seventy-one priests, scribes, and elders, presided over by the high priest.* For months the members of this court had determined their course of action against Jesus. As so often in human history, men are condemned before they have had a trial, judged before they have had an opportunity to face their accusers,

68

so here. Jesus must die. The chief justice had advised his associates before any trial had been held, *that is was expedient that one man should die for the people.*[3]

THE TRIAL: A TRAVESTY

The trial is held, but what a travesty on justice! While Jerusalem is sleeping, the court is called into session. In the dark hours of the night the palace of the high priest is well lighted. Such a session was illegal. But who cares about laws while Israel's Machiavelli is still in control! *Any means, however treacherous and despotic, are justifiable,* as long as they are employed to the end of maintaining a strong superchurch.

The court session opens. All eyes are upon the Defendant, who will be given no opportunity for defense. Witnesses of a sort were not lacking. *Though many false witnesses came, yet found they none* whose testimony could later procure the death sentence from the Procurator. At last two witnesses, unlike the others, were found whose testimony seemed to agree. *This fellow said, I am able to destroy the Temple of God, and to build it in three days.*

This was a lie. He had not said: I am able to destroy. He had said, *Destroy ye this temple,* meaning they would do it. He had not said: "the Temple of God." He had said, *this temple,* meaning His own body. He had not said: "I will build it in three days." He had said, *In three days I will raise it up,* meaning, I will raise it to life. Twisted minds ever twist words to their purposes. Even the church, as in this trial, is often guilty of using the courtroom trick of shyster lawyer and prejudiced judge. And these were the *shepherds of Israel!*

69

Caiaphas rises in irritation. He is baffled. He knew *a man could not be sentenced to death for a boastful word*. There must be some other way to convict this man. Israel had no Fifth Amendment. That will help. Say, Prisoner, *what is it which these witness against Thee?* If witnesses against Him are lacking, let the Prisoner bring in His own *damnatory evidence*.

Jesus held His peace. What divine composure! Silence in the face of a great injustice! *As a sheep before her shearers is dumb, so He openeth not His mouth.*[4] The very silence irks the high priest. *I adjure Thee by the living God that Thou tell us whether Thou be the Christ, the Son of God.*

So, now we have it! Caiaphas is coming to the point. Here lies the diabolical undercurrent of all the opposition against the King. Now we're getting at the real issues involved in this case. The court wants to know, O Jesus, are You the *Son of God*, are You the Messiah?

The attacks of men against the person of the Christ sealed His lips in silence. But when men asked for truth, the halls of the Sanhedrin had to re-echo the thunder of His royal reply, *Thou hast said!* Silence here would have been a denial of His Sonship, a denial of His royal priesthood. He must reply, and He does reply. The church and the world to the end of time shall hear the claims of the Christ about Himself. Where this voice does not speak to men, there will be no voice speaking for men.

Thou hast said! Caiaphas heard that voice. Yes, Caiaphas, I am He for whom all Israel has been waiting these many centuries. I am He for whom the world has been waiting since Eden became a shambles. And, Caiaphas, I will tell you more, Hereafter you will see

70

Me, the Son of Man, sitting on the right hand of Power, and coming in the clouds of heaven.

That's too much for Caiaphas. He tears his garment, as was customary in those days when a great sorrow had overtaken a man, and he shouts: That's blasphemy! We need no witnesses! You've all heard Him; *What think ye?* He knew what they were thinking. Their thoughts were his thoughts. There was only one answer, *He is guilty of death!* In that death the true High Priest shall find His true glory.

How Low the High Priest!

There they stand, these two, over against each other, Caiaphas and Christ; the former, a shadow; the Latter, the substance. Caiaphas, a symbol; Christ, the fulfillment. Caiaphas, degenerated man; Christ, regenerating men. How low can the church and its representatives sink from the high and holy position assigned to them by God? The priesthood of Israel which Caiaphas so ingloriously represented had a glorious history behind it.

Who were the first priests of God? In ancient times they were the fathers of families. *Priest,* like *presbyter,* means *the older ones, the elder.* Before God ordained a priesthood in Israel, God's children were blessed by a priesthood from the beginning of the world. Adam was priest in his household. Noah, as priest of God, brought sacrifices for his family. In the homes of Abraham and Isaac and Jacob, who were the ministers of God there if not the patriarchs themselves? What a glorious priesthood they represent!

And then came the time when Israel in the days of the Exodus must be organized for its greatest potential of service to God. The Lord chose Aaron and his sons,

71

and after them their sons' sons, to be the priests of the Most High. What glory was attached to their work! They were the mediators, the middle-men, between God and Israel. God had appointed them to their office. God had assigned them their work. God had even designed their clothing. Once each year the high priest was to enter alone into the Holy of Holies, place incense upon the burning coals of fire in the censer he carried; take the blood of a bullock and sprinkle it upon the mercy seat seven times as a sin offering for himself; take the blood of a goat and sprinkle it upon the mercy seat seven times as a sin offering for the people. While serving thus, he must wear upon each shoulder an onyx stone, each engraved with the names of six of the tribes of Israel. Upon his breast he must wear a gold plate, set with four rows of precious stones, three in each row. Like a signet, they were to be engraved with the names of the Twelve Tribes.

What glory for Israel's priesthood, to make atonement for God's people, to carry their burdens on one's shoulder, to carry their very names on one's heart, to stand between God and His people and to plead their cause! Was there ever greater glory than this?

And then, add to all this the fact that every ceremony performed by the high priest was a Messianic prophecy in itself. Each in turn pointed forward to the coming of a greater High Priest, who would be both Officiant and Sacrifice, Priest of God and Lamb of God. *Oh, come, Oh, come, Immanuel!* Each high priest waited patiently, but with joyful anticipation, for His advent.

When the Messiah came to His Temple, the high priest knew Him not, or rather, knowing Him and having the evidences of His advent, he rejected Him. *He came unto His own, and His own received Him not.*[5] The glory had departed from Israel, from priests as well as from people.

A Better High Priest

Though this glory of the ancient priesthood had departed from Israel, God was preparing a far greater glory, which should be the heritage of His spiritual Israel, the believers of the New Testament times. That greater glory lay in the priesthood of the King ever Glorious.

But was Jesus a high priest? *It is evident that our Lord sprang out of Juda; of which tribe Moses spake nothing concerning priesthood.*[6] So says the writer to the Hebrews. Jesus was King, for He came out of Judah's tribe, was a Son of David and inherited David's throne, but was He priest? The Letter to the Hebrews gives the answer. In former days there were many priests and high priests, *because they were not suffered to continue by reason of death.*[7] But Jesus, *this Man, because He continueth ever, hath an unchangeable priesthood.* Yes, Jesus was a high priest.

And this is the glory of His priesthood, that it was divinely appointed. God chose Him to supersede the ancient priesthood, to have pre-eminence over the high priests of the Old Covenant. Christ did not arrogate to Himself something that was not given Him by His Father. *"Christ glorified not Himself to be made a high priest; but He that said unto Him, Thou art My Son, today have I begotten Thee.*[8]

This is the glory of His priesthood that it was prefigured in that mysterious Old Testament character,

73

Melchizedek, five hundred years before there was an ordained priesthood in Israel. King David confirmed God's choice of the Messiah as high priest when he wrote, *The Lord hath sworn . . . Thou art a Priest forever after the order of Melchizedek.*[9]

This is the glory of His priesthood, that it was clothed with the spotless garment of sinlessness. The world needed such a High Priest, *who is holy, harmless, undefiled, separate from sinners, and made higher than the heavens.*[10] That spotless One was Christ Jesus.

This is the glory of His priesthood, that it has brought God in all His loving-kindness down to men. The King ever Glorious descends from His majestic throne, comes down to us, becomes one of us. *We have not a high priest which cannot be touched with the feeling of our infirmities, but was in all points tempted like as we are, yet without sin.*[11] This sympathetic King is our High Priest, our Brother.

This is the glory of His priesthood, that as our Brother He can do for us what the ancient high priests could not do for Israel. In all the history of the world God could choose no other to reconcile the world unto Himself. God could not use Adam. Adam had sinned. He could use neither Noah nor Abraham. They had sinned. He could use neither Moses nor Aaron. They had sinned. He could use neither Peter nor Paul. They had sinned. He could not use the Virgin Mary. Let us remind ourselves in the mystifying madness of the present Marian Year that she, too, had sinned. There was but One whom God could use to crush forever the curse that rested on man because of his sin, *Jesus Christ, the Righteous.*

74

This is not just a Lutheran pastor trying to weave something about the Christ that was not there in reality. The holy Bible long ago wove those holy vestments for Christ's glorious priesthood. *It behooved Him to be made like unto His brethren, that He might be a merciful and faithful High Priest in things pertaining to God, to make reconciliation for the sins of the people.*[12] There it is in all its Gospel simplicity! *Reconciled!* O glorious truth! *Reconcile* means *to unite again.* Sin separated us from God, but the blood of the High Priest once more unites us with God. We can sit down with God in friendly meeting, for we have been brought together by Jesus, the better High Priest.

Is He Your High Priest?

He was not the High Priest to those in the Sanhedrin, or to those who stood about in the courtroom. They treated Him like the scum of the earth. They spit upon His holy countenance. They played a game with Him. Having blindfolded Him, they hit Him with the palms of their hands and then shouted, *Prophesy unto us, Thou Christ, Who is he that smote Thee?*[13]

Thou needst not answer, O Lamb of God. We know. It was I who smote Thee, I and my parents and my children. Our sins, which are many, brought this woe on Thee. We spit upon Thee with our vileness. We smote Thee with the evil of our heart, our head, our hands. O forgive us, Thou holy Son of God!

Friend, you have come into our chapel as a visitor, to worship with us. I know you not. I know not the deep needs of your life, your ambitions, and your longings. But this I know, the King ever Glorious longs to be

75

united with you. As your High Priest He has been praying for you that you might come. As your High Priest He has broken down the impenetrable wall of your sin, which separated you from God. Come as you are, with all your sins. By His mercy those sins are now forgiven. By His grace He invites you to accept Him in faith as your Savior. Everything has been accomplished to make your eternal salvation sure. Pray fervently: Open Thou mine eyes, that I may see Thee in Thy glory.

And those of you who have heard this story through the many Lententides of the past, what will it mean to you? Go home rejoicing. The King has once again brought you His message of love. Through the blood of the High Priest your guilt is washed away. Your conscience is now at rest. There is peace with God. Out of that peace there flows to you comfort in your sorrows, hope in your fears, and life in the midst of death.

Out of that peace there will flow into your life the power to reflect in your every word and action the glory of the Savior's priesthood. *Ye are . . . a royal priesthood.*[14] Your heart is now a royal heart; it thinks the King's thoughts after Him. Your lips are now royal lips; they speak the King's language. Your hands are now royal hands; they do the King's work. Your feet are now royal feet; they walk the King's pathway. Your ears are now royal ears; they hear only the voice of the King. Your eyes are now brilliant with royalty's luster; they shine only for the King.

In this you are different from all the world. You are both king and priest. What brought the change? Not you, but Christ in you. The High Priest of God has won in you a priest for His service. As priest of God you sacrifice — sacrifice time and talent and treasure for the holy cause of His kingdom. As priest of God you stand daily as intercessor for all the world before the Almighty, praying that He might open human hearts to His Gospel.

> *For so the whole round earth is every way*
> *Bound by gold chains about the feet of God.*[15]

This is the glory of the priesthood of our King ever Glorious, He has won you! And by you, God's priest, the whole world shall be bound to the feet of God. Amen.

VIII. THE GLORY OF HIS PASSION

And after this, Joseph of Arimathea, being a disciple of Jesus, but secretly for fear of the Jews, besought Pilate that he might take away the body of Jesus; and Pilate gave him leave. He came, therefore, and took the body of Jesus. And there came also Nicodemus, which at the first came to Jesus by night, and brought a mixture of myrrh and aloes, about an hundred pound weight. Then took they the body of Jesus, and wound it in linen clothes with the spices, as the manner of the Jews is to bury. Now, in the place where He was crucified there was a garden, and in the garden a new sepulcher, wherein was never man yet laid. There laid they Jesus, therefore, because of the Jews' preparation day; for the sepulcher was nigh at hand. — John 19:38-42.

A strange feeling comes over us as we prepare to speak to you at the vesper hour of this holy day, Good Friday. There is an emotion within us that we can hardly explain to ourselves, much less to others. We have often made this experience in life, that when our closest friends have passed into the great eternity, human language seemed so superfluous. Our lips were sealed because God had already spoken His own language. It is difficult to say anything while we stand at the grave of one whose hand we have touched, whose life was so intimately intertwined with our own. And if we find it difficult to utter the deepest thoughts of our heart as we lay to rest those who were close to us in life, what can one say at the burial of Him who shall be close to us in all eternity.

What is there that human language can add to the record of the burial of the King ever Glorious? What can one say at the funeral of God's Son? Better far my tongue were dumb than that I should parade my puny preaching before men, when God has already written the sermon for His Son in blood. Far better if I would merely read to you God's record, and leave my preaching unpreached.

And yet, God would have us speak on this day. *Preach the Word!*[1] He says. There is a message that men must hear on this day, or they die eternally. It is the message of God's eternal love for man. Without that love Good Friday is a gory and gruesome scene. But with that love the cross sends forth its heavenly harmony, *komm, suesser Tod! — Come, Sweet Death!* It is the King who invites Death to take Him. By His death shall the lives of His people be made sweet. In His death shall be consummated all the glory of His Passion.

THE GLORY OF HIS PASSION

Most of you are familiar with the changing scenes of that first Good Friday. The church had condemned the Christ. To execute Him was not within their power. Early in the morning they rush Him to Pilate, who should pass sentence of death upon Him. Pilate suspects the truth. He tries to get rid of the case by sending King Jesus to King Herod. That doesn't work. He gets the case back again. He tortures Jesus and thus attempts to arouse pity for Him in the hearts of the people. That

79

doesn't work either. He tries to free himself from this case in which he is enmeshed by giving the people a choice. He places the Christ next to Barabbas, whose hands were stained with blood. *Whom will ye that I release unto you?* Surely they will choose Jesus! But it doesn't work. Give us Barabbas! — What about your King? — *Crucify Him!* No, Pilate, that water will not wash away your guilt!

They lead Him to Calvary, bearing His cross. *And there they crucified Him.*[2] Need I tell you the horrors of such a death? In His agony He prays, *Father, forgive them!* Priests and people mock Him. Rulers and riffraff deride Him. Hardened soldiers and hardened malefactors taunt Him. Out of heaven there comes a darkness that engulfs Him. *My God, my God, why?* Ask not, Thou Son of Man, Thou knowest. — Yes, I know. *It is finished.*

Father, into Thy hands I commend My Spirit.[3] Silently He bows His head and gives His soul into the hands of His heavenly Father. His body is a corpse. This is death. Is this not the end? Oh, no, this is not the end. Look to the top of the cross. Do you see that sign? It was placed there on Pilate's order, in three languages. What does it say? *THIS IS THE KING,*[4] as Luke has it. If He is King ever Glorious, then His life and His death had a purpose.

LIFE THROUGH HIS DEATH

The glory of His Passion, of which death was merely the climax, was that it restored to fallen men their lost heritage of life, spiritual life here and eternal life there. Sin had wrapped its ugly coils about man and crushed him to death. Sin's destructive venom coursed through man's veins from cradle to grave. Hear how Saint Paul describes sin's progress. *By one man sin entered into the world, and death by sin; and so death passed upon all men, for that all have sinned.*[5] Through Adam God's beautiful creation became one vast cemetery. Not life, but death became man's heritage. That's how Job puts it: *I know that Thou wilt bring me to death, and to the house appointed for all living.*[6] No power on earth can reclaim life from the clutches of death. *We must needs die, and are as water spilt on the ground, which cannot be gathered up again,*[7] says the wise woman of Tekoah to King David.

To cope with death, to restore life to men, required the powers of heaven. This was the purpose of the coming of the King. Through His death life would be restored to men. *I am come that they might have life, and that they might have it more abundantly,*[8] says Jesus. The disciples did not understand this. Matthew tells us that six days before the Transfiguration Jesus gave them the first distinct prediction of His Passion and death. *From that time forth began Jesus to show unto His disciples how that He must . . . suffer many things . . . and be killed.*[9] Peter replied, *Be it far from Thee, Lord.* Jesus turned upon Peter, *Get thee behind Me, Satan.* So certain was Jesus of the purpose of His coming that any interference with the divine plan of redemption became to Him an evidence of satanic influence.

Thy life was given for me, Thy blood for me was shed. This is more than poetic fancy. This is divine truth. My life was a failure. By my sins I broke God's holy Law. But the Law had to be kept, or there could be no salvation for me. Neither I nor all the world could keep that Law. For this problem God had an answer.

When the fullness of the time was come, God sent forth His Son . . . made under the Law, to redeem them that were under the Law.[10] Do you see what happened? To get you and me out from under the heavy burden of the Law, God put Jesus under that Law. He lifted it up, He fulfilled its every requirement, He kept all the Commandments perfectly. Now God looks at us as though we had kept the Law. That's what Paul means by *redeeming them that were under the Law.* Redemption means substitution; the Just lived His life for the unjust. Yes, *Thy life was given for me.*

But more. *Thy blood for me was shed.* This, too, is divine truth. Transgressions against God's Law had to be punished. Had God not exacted a penalty for the sins of men, then God's justice would have been violated; God would stop being God. I could not pay that penalty. My guilt is so enormous that I would have had to keep on paying throughout eternity, and never be finished with the task. But God is Love. In love He found a Substitute. Read it and rejoice on this Good Friday! Here is the glory of the Passion, the suffering, of our King. *It is not possible that the blood of bulls and of goats should take away sins. . . . But this Man . . . by one offering hath perfected forever them that are sanctified.*[11] Do you see what happened? The King offered Himself as a sacrifice to pay your and my penalty. All the tormenting wounds of His body, the hellish agonies of His soul, they were all ours. We should have suffered thus. This is the glory of His Passion, that by the death of the King mankind has been declared free. Yes, *Thy blood was shed for me.* That is why you see the King at the close of His Passion, nailed to the accursed tree, dead.

There is, however, another element of glory that attaches to the Passion of the King. The Gospel of this Passion wins the hearts of men through its own power. *It is the power of God unto salvation to everyone that believeth.*[12] It was so on that first Good Friday many centuries ago.

At three o'clock the Savior had commended His soul into the hands of His Father. His soul and body were now at rest. We are not told whether Caiaphas or some priest, or any of His enemies for that matter, gave even a passing thought to what would happen to His body, beyond the fact that the Jews asked Pilate to hasten the death of the three crucified men on Calvary, because the next day was a holy day. Perhaps they thought: Let Him hang there. If His body must be taken down, let the soldiers handle that. They'll throw the three bodies into some pit.

There were others who still loved Him, even in death. Let us step close to the cross and observe them. Among those who are lingering on Golgotha we recognize a few women and a man. The man is Joseph, a man of wealth and social position. He came from Arimathea, but seems to have had his home in Jerusalem, for he had already made provision for his own burial. He had selected a grave on the hillside near Golgotha, in a garden. What are his thoughts under the cross? Is he perhaps wondering why no one seems to be making preparations to give Jesus a decent burial? Did Jesus not have some friends, especially those twelve men who traveled through the country with Him? Joseph looks in all directions from Golgotha, but all that meets his eye is the crowd of the curious returning to the city. No one is coming up the road toward him. Where are His friends? Not one to bury Him?

He is resolved what to do. This burial shall be his responsibility. Joseph rushes into the city. He finds Pilate. *He went in boldly* [13] *. . . and begged the body of Jesus.* — Pilate marvels: So soon dead? — The centurion is called to confirm it. Yes, Pilate, He's dead! — Permission granted!

It is getting late. Hastening from the courthouse to the market, Joseph quickly buys fine linen and hastens back to Golgotha. He is about to begin his labor of love. He looks at the still form and wonders how best to take it down. Behind him stands a silent, kindred friend, with a heavy bag containing a *mixture of myrrh and aloes, about an hundred pound weight,* at his feet. Joseph turns about. His eyes meet the eyes of Nicodemus. These two had met before. — Nicodemus, you too? — Yes, I!

Here they stand beneath the cross, these two, mute evidences of the power of the Gospel, eloquent evidences of the glory of Christ's Passion. *Thus Jesus by being lifted up is already drawing men unto Him. These Jewish aristocrats first confess Him in the hour of His deepest degradation.* Wealth and wisdom unite in their devotion to the crucified Love. *Then took they the body of Jesus and wrapped it in the clean linen cloth and wound it in linen cloths with the spices, as the manner of the Jews is to bury.*

With bleeding hearts the few women who had remained step closer. With tender hands they assist in the holiest work ever performed by man; they prepare the body of the God-Man for burial. But where shall they bury Him? Joseph looks up. He points to the side of the hill, to a garden. They see an empty tomb. — It is mine. It shall be His! — The precious burden is borne down the hillside, placed into the tomb, one last look of love, and the heavy stone rolls into place.

That stone writes *Finis* to His Passion, but not *Finis* to His glory. Never again shall men look upon the humiliated Christ. A rich man and a wise man were the last to see Him thus. After today, men will see Him only with the eyes of faith, see Him in the glory of His Passion, see Him as the King ever Glorious.

A Vision That Penetrates

What brought Joseph and Nicodemus to Golgotha? Their common faith in Jesus. Their faith hurdled all obstacles.

How came the rich man to be there? Jesus had once said, *It is easier for a camel to go through the eye of a needle than for a rich man to enter into the kingdom of God.*[14] Joseph knew that Jesus had no earthly wealth to share with him, no mansion to which He might invite him, no business contacts which might prove advantageous to him. Why then had Joseph come? Because he had faith's vision, which penetrated the garment of Christ's humiliation and saw Him as the King ever Glorious. Jesus, the Messiah, could give Joseph what he needed most, spiritual food for his daily life, forgiveness for his sins, peace for his troubled conscience, rest in the hour of death. All this Joseph could not buy in any marketplace with all his wealth. On Golgotha he received it by grace, through faith, *without money and without price.*[15]

85

How came the wise man to be there? Jesus had once said to him, *except a man be born again, he cannot see the kingdom of God.*[16] Nicodemus knew that Jesus could bring him no earthly honor and glory, He could add nothing to his social stature, He would add nothing to his store of worldly wisdom. Why then had Nicodemus come? Because by the grace of God he had been reborn. He had experienced the transforming power of the Gospel in his life. Faith's vision had penetrated the humanity of the King and had grasped His deity. On Golgotha Nicodemus exchanged a few grains of sand for the ocean strand of divine wisdom. The Passion of the King had accomplished this. That is its glory.

The Veil on the Cross

The miraculous transformation of Joseph and Nicodemus which we have seen on Calvary will ever accompany the message of Christ's Passion. What happened there will happen here. It will happen in New York and Chicago and San Francisco, and here among us in New Orleans. It is true, God said, *My Word . . . shall not return unto Me void.*[17] But the Gospel cannot get through to the hearts of men as long as they feel no need for that Gospel. God will not heal as long as men do not recognize their wounds. God will not save until men see their sin.

As you came into the narthex of our chapel this evening, you beheld through the open door the striking simplicity of our altar, stripped of its sacred vessels, and adorned only by crucifix and black paraments. As you stepped closer and beheld the black veil upon the cruci-fix, you gasped. Some of you whispered in hushed voices: Who did that? May I give you God's answer.

Thou art the man. Who veiled that cross on Calvary in black? You and I. Who drove the King ever Glorious into His holy Passion? You and I. Who killed the Prince of Life? You and I. This is the tragedy of our irreligious age with its religious sentimentality, that men no longer want to be reminded of the blackness of their hearts and lives. They want peace when there is no peace. They want God without godliness. They want religion without repentance. It is about time we learned to gasp at our sins.

I am fully aware of the fact, without your reminding me, that the veil we have placed upon the crucifix tonight adds nothing to the power of the Gospel, adds nothing to the message of the Cross. But this I know, even though you forget all I've said tonight, you will not easily forget the sight which greeted your eyes, the veil on the cross. God has tried to get at your heart through your ears for years. You've blocked His way. Perhaps tonight He will get at your heart through your eyes. By means of a simple Good Friday ceremony that has come down to us through the centuries and even today is observed in hundreds of our Christian churches, may God teach you once more to pray:

> *Ah! I also and my sin*
> *Wrought Thy deep affliction;*
> *This indeed the cause hath been*
> *Of Thy crucifixion.*[18]

When you have prayed thus, then the King ever Glorious comes to you in the glory of His Passion. He embraces you and all the world in His redeeming love. He assures you, *This I did for thee.* Hell with its torments is gone. The Law with its curse is removed. Death with its dread is swallowed up in victory. Sin with its power over human lives is broken. Oh, come then, ye rich, ye wise, ye poor, ye ignorant, young and old, men and women, boys and girls, come and remove with us the veil from Calvary's cross, and let it shine forth in all the glory of the King's Passion. Come and sing:

In the Cross of Christ I glory
Tow'ring o'er the wrecks of time.
By His wondrous death and Passion
Jesus made His heaven mine.

Amen

IX. THE GLORY OF HIS PROMISES

Now, the next day, that followed the day of the prepara-
tion, the chief priests and Pharisees came together unto
Pilate, saying, Sir, we remember that that deceiver said
while He was yet alive, After three days I will rise
again. Command therefore that the sepulcher be made
sure until the third day, lest His disciples come by night
and steal Him away, and say unto the people, He is
risen from the dead; so the last error shall be worse
than the first. Pilate said unto them, Ye have a watch;
go your way, make it as sure as ye can. So they went,
and made the sepulcher sure, sealing the stone, and
setting a watch. — Matthew 27:62-66.

It is Easter Eve. In this vesper hour of Holy Saturday
I should like to take you by the hand and lead you once
more to the tomb in the garden where lies the King ever
Glorious. We have spent many blessed moments during
this Lententide in the holy companionship of this King.
Our lives have been enriched, our faith deepened, and
our hope for a blessed eternity strengthened. Once more
we desire to be near Him. We cannot see Him. The
stone has sealed Him away from our view. We cannot
speak to Him. His body is cold in death. We cannot
hear His voice. His lips are silent.

And yet it seems as though He were speaking to us. We cannot escape the feeling that all about us there is a voice that comes from out the tomb. We are perplexed. We look about, and — ah! yes, there it is! It is the voice of His enemies. Though the King is dead, yet He speaks through those who hated Him. Though they hated Him, yet must they proclaim

THE GLORY OF HIS PROMISES

This is the thought that shall engage us in our meditation on this Easter Eve.

It was a Sabbath day, that day after the Savior had been laid into the tomb, a day of rest. The stirring events of the previous day had come to an end. The unthinking multitudes who had played their minor parts in the drama on Calvary could readjust their emotions, that is, if there were any sensibilities left in them. Pilate could go on without any readjustment. For him it was business as usual. He was accustomed to this sort of sordid thing. The priests and the high priests could rest, for their "enemy" was dead. The disciples could — could what? What could they do? Their Friend was dead.

Promises Forgotten

Is it not strange that no writer of Holy Writ tells us what the disciples did on that Holy Saturday, when the Savior lay in the grave? How can it be? These men had valiantly affirmed, *Though I should die with Thee, yet will I not deny Thee.* They all had said that. *Likewise also said all the disciples.*[1] If they could not watch with Him in life, could they not at least watch at His grave?

Where are these brave men? It was an act of mercy that the Holy Spirit pulled down the curtain on this inglorious scene. Future ages should remember these men not by the thoughts and deeds of this day, but by the thoughts and deeds of which they became capable in the days that lay ahead. The very silence of Scripture about them emphasizes their doubt and fear and confusion, and their forgetfulness.

They had forgotten His promises made throughout the three years of instruction. They had forgotten every promise of power made in every miracle they had witnessed in those three years. They had heard His Sermon on the Mount, *Take no thought for your life.*[2] On this day they could remember no sermon. They *beheld His glory* on the Mount of Transfiguration. On this day they could remember no glory. On the last journey to Jerusalem they had heard Him say, *We go up to Jerusalem, and . . . the Son of Man shall be . . . spitefully entreated . . . and they shall . . . put Him to death; and the third day He shall rise again.*[3] *Jerusalem* and *death* they remembered, but the promise, *He shall rise again,* they had forgotten. Jesus had often explained the Old Testament promises of a Messiah to them, but they had forgotten that every Prophet of old pointed not to a dead King, but to the King who shall live forever. How treacherous a memory that fails in time of need!

It were far better for us on this day to leave the curtain where the Holy Spirit placed it, and to look at ourselves. Each day of our life this inglorious scene is reborn in us, as we forget the promises of our loving Lord. In our complex living of today there is much to make us restless, to be sure. Have we forgotten His

91

promise, *Come unto Me . . . and I will give you rest.*[4] The specter of broken health or breaking business drives the shaft of fear deep into the hearts of men. Have we forgotten His promise? *Fear thou not, for I am with thee; be not dismayed, for I am thy God; I will strengthen thee; yea, I will help thee.*[5] We go through life like forgotten men and women, friendless and forlorn. Have we forgotten His promise that He will be a Friend to us and crown our lives *with loving-kindness and tender mercies?*[6] We have enemies. Have we forgotten what the Psalmist says about Israel in its day of need? *He suffered no man to do them wrong; yea, He reproved kings for their sakes.*[7]

But why should I go on with this catalog of forgetfulness? You and I must surely recognize that the ultimate cause of all our sorrow is our sin. But God has a solution for the problem of sin. He took our guilt and placed it upon His Son Jesus. *He was wounded for our transgressions.*[8] That took from us the heavy load we could not carry and placed it upon the shoulders of the King. If that load is gone, then the weight of its sorrow has also been removed. Now there can be no doubt and fear and confusion. If only the disciples had remembered!

If only you and I would remember! From today on let us learn to take God at His word. Let us daily open the King's Book and there read the glory of His promises. Let us believe God when He brings the light of His promises into the dark corners of our lives. Heaven is ours through the pardon of the King. Earth and all her benedictions are ours by the grace of the King. *All things are yours.* Let us believe the King.

There were those who did not believe the King, but they remembered. Matthew speaks of them in the text. It is the only text of the Bible which makes mention of the events of Holy Saturday. The dead King was still a disturbing element in the lives of some people in Jerusalem — disturbing, because He had promised His followers so much. Even though the followers forgot, the enemies remembered.

Their remembrance stirs them to unholy action. Chief priests and Pharisees rush to Pilate with a great discovery. *Sir, we remember that that deceiver said . . . After three days I will rise again.*[9] What's your hurry and your worry, Caiaphas? If He was a deceiver, of what are you afraid? He can harm you none. He's dead! The deed is done. Your little word has felled Him! Come, Caiaphas, be reasonable. See how He lies there — impotent, lifeless, dead. Is death not sufficient guard for the dead? Do you need the impotent living to keep the dead behind death's door?

Or is it maybe possible, Caiaphas, that among all the thousands in Jerusalem who believed not the King, you are the only one on this day of rest who is restless? Restless, perhaps, because you've had more than shreds of evidence that this despised Carpenter — no, you called Him *deceiver* — is still King ever Glorious? Caiaphas, there's not much time to lose. Get away from Pilate. Go to one of your associate judges in the Sanhedrin, Nicodemus by name; he could tell you many things about this King which you have never heard. He could tell you about his midnight visit with the King more than three years ago, a visit that changed his whole life. He

93

could tell you that he was the first to hear those glorious words from the lips of the King: *God so loved the world that He gave His only-begotten Son, that whosoever believeth in Him should not perish, but have everlasting life.*[10] Surely you must remember the words of Nicodemus spoken many months ago in your council chamber, when you had sent out the officers to arrest Jesus, but they came back empty-handed, *Doth our Law judge any man before it hear him?* [11] O Caiaphas, you have heard Him, but you have not heard the last of Him. Tomorrow you shall hear more. Come out at dawn, and you shall see the heavens ablaze with the glory of His promise, *in three days I will raise it up.*

But why should I address Caiaphas? He is not here. He has gone to his place. I speak thus because all about us in our community there still live the children of Caiaphas, men and women who have eyes, but they see not, ears have they, but they hear not, minds they have, but they think not, hearts they have, but they believe not. They have not seen the glory of the fulfilled promises of the King. Who shall tell them the story of His glory?

Our heart was grieved last year on Holy Saturday, when the newspapers announced the sermon topics for the Easter services in the churches of our city. Among them was this topic by a Protestant pastor, *Why We Do Not Believe in the Resurrection.* Here is Caiaphas come back to life! Pilate, give us your soldiers. We'll make sure that there won't be a *last error* that could *be worse than the first.*

Ye have a watch; go your way, make it as sure as ye can — if you can. Forward! March, you soldiers! We have a job to do. Out to the tomb of the King of the

94

Jews! The King is dead! Long may He stay dead! He promised His followers He would rise. He shall not rise! It must not happen! It cannot happen!

But It Did Happen!

Beloved, but it did happen! You have noticed that our little chancel on this Easter Eve already reflects the glory of His fulfilled promise. For this vesper service the altar is already adorned with its Easter beauty, the white paraments, the white lilies, the glowing candles. The black veil has been removed from the crucifix. On this night we are no longer living in the gloom of Good Friday, but in the glories of the Easter dawn.

All this is but a simple liturgical device to bring to the eye that which the heart already holds with firm conviction, the glory of a promise fulfilled. Let the iconoclasts call the rich heritage of our Lutheran liturgical practices *Roman!* As every instructor of children teaches through the eye as well as the ear, so we will not be deterred in our method of teaching the children of God. Who would rob us of this in view of the Lord's permissive encouragement, *All things are yours?*

Far more glorious, however, than all the beautiful chancel adornment on Easter Eve is the adornment of a Christian life that goes out into this dark world of unbelief and proclaims by word and deed: It did happen. Caiaphas dreaded the thought that disciples would go out and *say unto the people, He is risen from the dead.* Let our world rejoice that you have come and have proclaimed the glory of His promise.

Who will tell these people who are going down into eternal damnation because of their unforgiven sins, that there is a Savior who will pardon? These people of our community need the message that only you can bring. They will not come into our churches. They refuse to read the tracts and devotional booklets we hand them. When the radio announces those three magnetic words, *The Lutheran Hour*, they quickly turn to another station. When our Lutheran program, *This Is the Life*, appears on their television set, they quickly select another channel, because this is not their life. How is Christ going to get close to these people if not through you? The glorious promise of the King, the promise of salvation only through faith in the blood of the Lamb, will remain unfulfilled in the lives of these our unbelieving neighbors, unless you and I accept as our Easter motto, *Each One Reach One*.

You need no college degree to tell a man that his life without God and without Christ is leading him to hell. You need no seminary course to tell a man that God made a promise to take away this curse of sin through the suffering and death of Jesus. You need no eloquence to tell a man that God has kept all His promises and will keep them in all eternity.

And if your tongue be dumb, then let your life do the preaching. Let men see by the love of your deeds, the kindness in your words, the hope in your hearts, that the King ever Glorious lives in you. Let men know that, *being, then, made free from sin, ye became the servants of righteousness.*[12] This is the strength we pray for on the eve of Easter. It did happen — it happened in us! His promise did not fail us.

This is the glory of the promise of the King ever Glorious. In the light of that promise we await the dawn of Easter. Amen.

X. THE GLORY OF HIS PEACE

Then He said unto them, O fools, and slow of heart to believe all that the Prophets have spoken! Ought not Christ to have suffered these things and to enter into His glory? And beginning at Moses and all the Prophets, He expounded unto them in all the Scriptures the things concerning Himself. And they drew nigh unto the village whither they went; and He made as though He would have gone further. But they constrained Him, saying, Abide with us; for it is toward evening, and the day is far spent. And He went in to tarry with them. And it came to pass, as He sat at meat with them, He took bread, and blessed it, and brake, and gave to them. And their eyes were opened, and they knew Him; and He vanished out of their sight. And they said one to another, Did not our heart burn within us while He talked with us by the way, and while He opened to us the Scriptures? And they rose up the same hour, and returned to Jerusalem, and found the Eleven gathered together, and them that were with them, saying, The Lord is risen indeed, and hath appeared to Simon. And they told what things were done in the way, and how He was known of them in breaking of bread. And as they thus spake, Jesus Himself stood in the midst of them and saith unto them, Peace be unto you.

Luke 24:25-36

In the name of Him who *hath on His vesture and on His thigh a name written, KING OF KINGS AND LORD OF LORDS.*[1] Amen.

Easter is a great climax. It is the climax in the life of the King ever Glorious, who went forth to do battle with the enemies of God and man. He returned from that battle, *all His raiment stained with blood,*[2] but in His hand the crown of victory. Saint John the Divine saw the King in the glory of His victory, sitting upon a white horse, His vesture *dipped in blood,*[3] but inscribed with the name *King of Kings.* This is He whom Saint Paul called *the blessed and only Potentate, the King of Kings.*[4] This is He whom Isaiah saw in prophecy as *the Prince of Peace.*[5] This is He of whom the angelic host sang on the night of the holy Nativity, *Peace on earth.* Of Him all Christendom sings today on the feast of the Resurrection, *Christ is risen! Alleluia! Christ is risen from the dead.*

What a contrast, our Easter of today and the Easter nineteen hundred years ago! Today we look out upon our world and behold the countless thousands in cathedrals and chapels, on hillsides and along lake shores, out in the country and in the city, worshiping the King. The mighty chorus of Christian voices in all lands rises in a tremendous crescendo, *Hallelujah, He is risen indeed!* It was not so twenty centuries ago. The followers of the King were few in number. Their voices were silenced by grief and fear. They were perplexed, they trembled; their worst fears had come true, *He is not here.* How can men have peace in such an atmosphere? But peace did come to them, the peace that *passeth all understanding,* when they met the King. May the Spirit grant us true Easter joy as we behold Him in His glory.

98

THE GLORY OF HIS PEACE

Easter was a very sad day for the followers of the Savior. The events of the past days had benumbed their senses. They were perplexed. Their hopes had been shattered. Added to this was their sense of guilt. All of them had made such wonderful promises of loyalty, yet none of them had kept the promise. Their fears made them traitors even on Easter morn. Locked doors are the symbol of their search for security.

The story of the women who had been early at the grave only added to their confusion. This is what had happened. Very early in the morning, while it was still dark, Mary Magdalene and Joanna and Mary, the mother of James, and several other women went out to the garden of the tomb to complete the work of burial which had been interrupted by the Sabbath on Friday evening. On the way they discuss the problem of the heavy stone at the entrance. Upon their arrival at the grave they notice that the stone is rolled away. Without investigating the reason, Mary Magdalene runs back into the city to tell Peter. While she is on her errand the other women enter the tomb. Instead of finding Jesus they find two angels, who proclaim the glad news that Christ is risen. *Behold the place where they laid Him. But go your way, tell His disciples.*[6] Surely this must bring them the real Easter joy! But it doesn't.

They went out quickly and fled from the sepulcher, for they trembled . . . for they were afraid. Fear on Easter! What a spectacle!

In the meantime Mary Magdalene had brought the news to Peter. He and John run to the grave and find the linen burial cloths wrapped and lying separately. *As yet they knew not the Scripture, that He must rise.*[7] They go back to their home. Mary Magdalene is still in the garden. She stands weeping at the tomb of the resurrection. She stoops down to look more closely through her tears. She sees the two angels. They ask, *Woman, why weepest thou?*[8] She notices someone standing behind her. He, too, asks, *Woman, why weepest thou?*[9] — *Sir . . . tell me where thou hast laid Him.* — *Mary!* — *Master!*

Mary again runs into the city, this time to tell *the disciples that she had seen the Lord.*[10] When she came to them, *they mourned and wept. And they, when they had heard that He was alive, and had been seen of her, believed not.*[11] How can there be Easter joy and peace when there is no faith!

While all this was happening, the other women were still on the way back to the city. With them it was fear mixed with joy. Jesus appears to them on the way and says, *All hail! . . . Be not afraid; go tell My brethren.*[12] The women *told these things unto the Apostles. And their words seemed to them as idle tales, and they believed them not.*[13]

But there is still more to this story of unbelief. In the afternoon of this glorious day two men from the wider circle of Christ's disciples are on their way to the town of Emmaus. The Emmaus road was no road of peace to them. They *talked,* they *communed,* they *reasoned,* there was a lively discussion about *all these things which had happened.* Suddenly they are joined by a Stranger who immediately joins in their conversation and asks for the reason of their sad hearts, sad faces, sad words with each other. One of them, Cleopas, answers: What! Are you the only stranger in these parts who hasn't heard what has happened these last days? — The Stranger replies: No! I haven't heard. What things? — Both of the disciples burst out with a story that is devoid of Easter glory. It has all the gloom of Good Friday about it. — It's about Jesus of Nazareth we've been talking. A Prophet He was, mighty in word and deed . . . Our priests and rulers took Him, condemned Him, and crucified Him . . . We thought He would redeem Israel . . . That was three days ago . . . Now this morning . . . some of our women were at the grave . . . They didn't find Him . . . Some angels said He was alive . . . Some of our men went down to find out . . . Him they saw not . . . What do you make of it? . . . Do you think it could have happened? . . . But after all, facts are facts, even in religion . . . Nobody saw Him.

O foolish men, how stupid not to believe what the Prophets have said about this Jesus! Didn't Moses and Isaiah and all the others say that this would happen? Didn't they say He would be born in Bethlehem? It happened. Didn't they say He would flee to Egypt? It happened. Didn't they say He would perform great miracles on the sick and the dead? It happened. Didn't they say He would give His *back to the smiters*,[14] would suffer thirst, would hang between criminals, would see men gamble for His robe, would die on the cross, would be buried in a rich man's grave? It all happened. Didn't the Prophets say He would again enter into His glory? If all the rest happened, why not this? Oh, you two Emmaus disciples, you are sad, for you believe not; you have no joy, for you accept not; you have no peace within yourselves, for you have no faith!

101

Here is Easter's first great lesson. The road to peace is the road of faith. The Emmaus road is still the road which is being traveled by many in our day. To those sitting in the agonies of their smiting conscience Christ is still dead. They have not in faith accepted His word of pardon; *Son, be of good cheer, thy sins be forgiven thee.*[15] To those sitting amid their fears of the future, Christ is still dead. They have not in faith accepted His word of encouragement: *Be of good cheer, I have overcome the world.*[16] To those sitting in their little ship of life, fearful of the specters they see on troubled waters and hear in contrary winds, Christ is still dead. They have not in faith accepted His clear voice in the dead of night: *Be of good cheer; it is I; be not afraid.*[17] Truly, where there is no faith, men shall never find peace.

II. HE STILL LIVES AND LOVES

Men find that peace only when they learn that Christ still lives and loves. This is the way in which the Emmaus disciples found peace. When they met the Stranger on the road, *their eyes were holden that they should not know Him.* Christ could have appeared to them as He did to the Magdalene. But they had to learn their lesson first, the lesson of trusting the Word of God when it speaks to men. There would come a time in their lives when they had to walk by faith and not by sight. In this sightless walking of the future there would be but one light to guide them, the Word of God.

Beginning at Moses and all the Prophets, He expounded unto them in all the Scriptures the things concerning Himself. Until He had made them sure of the trustworthiness of Scripture, He could not reveal Him-

102

self. This would give them certainty in their religion. Their message to the world would be positive and faith-inspiring, He still lives and loves.

The manner in which they learned their lesson is told in a most tender way. It was evening. They had now reached their home. The Stranger acts *as though He would have gone further.* They plead with Him, *Abide with us, for it is toward evening, and the day is far spent.* Little did they know that their prayer would become the doorway to a heavenly peace. They are seated at the table. The Stranger takes the bread, blesses it, breaks it, and gives them to eat. In that moment *their eyes were opened, and they knew Him; and He vanished out of their sight.*

He still lives! The Scriptures had foretold it, angels had announced it, women had reported it, now they had seen it. *Did not our heart burn within us . . . while He opened to us the Scriptures?* Oh, may on this glorious day the hearts be burning within the countless throngs of millions, as the Scriptures are opened unto them in the message of the Resurrection! *Christ is risen!* This message will bring peace to men because it brings them certainty in religion. He still lives! That is the *keystone of Christianity.*

From Broadway and Main Street, from battlefield and prison, from factory and hospital, from prairie and mountainside, from the sunny South and frozen North, from ships at sea and boats on the bayou, there goes up the universal cry of men: Oh, how can I be sure of my salvation? If men would but walk once more the Emmaus road, they would find the simple answer to their searching question. He still lives and loves! He lives to demonstrate to all the world that He is God and Lord, King

ever Glorious. He was *declared to be the Son of God
. . . by the resurrection from the dead.*[18] He still lives,
to show us that He is God. *He was raised again for our
justification.*[19] He still lives, to show us that His work
of redeeming the world has been completed, that before
God we are now through His atoning blood declared just
and righteous. *Not by works of righteousness which we
have done, but according to His mercy He saved us.*[20]
He still lives, to show us that our works were insufficient
to save, but that His mercy has accomplished what was
impossible for man. Not man's character, not man's sacrifices and pilgrimages, not man's merit and good inten-
tions, but only the mercy of God stands as the open door
to heaven. That door was opened when Christ, our King,
came forth victoriously from the grave. He still lives!
Here is heaven's assurance that I may have certainty in
religion, the certainty that God for Christ's sake has forgiven my sin.

If He still lives, then He also still loves! The same
Bible that promised the world that the King would live,
also promised the world that the King would love. You
need this certainty in your daily life. *I have loved thee
with an everlasting love.*[21] I know that is hard for you
to believe. You have spent months in sickness, life has
dealt you many a hard blow, you go on from day to day,
surrounded by life's disappointments, your heartaches are
with you by day, and in the silent watches of the night
they do not leave you. You cry out: How can I believe
that God loves me still? Here is your answer. *Greater
love hath no man than this, that a man lay down his
life for his friends.*[22] On the cross Christ gave you the
greatest evidence of His love. On Easter morn He put

Heaven's stamp of approval on that love. If He lives, then He loves — He loves you.

Believe this with all your heart, then the highway to heaven will no longer be shrouded in the fog and mist of uncertainty. Accept this, then life with its misfortunes will no longer be a successive series of question marks. Cling to this, then eternity will hold no terrors, cemeteries will bring no disquieting thoughts, the Judgment and its verdict will no longer be a horrifying reality. Come back to Emmaus with us on this day of days, and behold the peace that came to hearts that burned with the knowledge that He still lives and loves. Pray fervently: O King ever Glorious, abide with us, and grant us Thy peace.

III. Peace of Heart Makes Restless Feet

The moment these disciples recognized the glorious truth which Jesus had imparted to them, the truth of His resurrection and the truth of His love, they left there upon the table their untouched and uneaten bread. Truth and certainty were supplying wings for their feet. They hastened out of Emmaus. They didn't say: We can't go now. It's dark outside. We'll wait until tomorrow. No, the good news cannot wait. The Emmaus road had become a road of peace. Now it must become a road of action. That road had been dark for them during the day, now it shall be made bright by them in the night. The slumbering pebbles and dust of the road must be awakened when men have passed through portals of prayer and become messengers of peace. Highways of happiness will be built for other men to travel if once the construction crew has met the King. While other

105

men are sleeping, they will rush into the job. For them there is no tomorrow. Their work must be done now, today!

Do we realize the implications of all this for our small congregation? Do we realize what this Easter message means for your life and mine? When God brings to human hearts the comfort of peace through the resurrection of Christ from the dead, those hearts make restless feet, or men lose their souls. God planted this church here to win souls for heaven. That is true. But He also planted it to gain co-workers for the King.

Let us get a few things straight. This congregation was not organized so that you would have a church closer to your home. It is not our mission policy to plant another church in an area which can be and is being served by one of our congregations. That would be squandering God's men and money while the rest of the world is going to hell. No Lutheran who can get to his church in thirty minutes has a right to request another church so that he can get there in ten minutes. God didn't tell us to cut the driving time of our members. He did tell us, however, to cut the terrific rate at which Satan is driving souls to eternal perdition. This church was planted here in this area because there are hundreds and hundreds of people living throughout this community who have not heard of the King in all His glory. There is no peace in their hearts because they have not heard of the glorious peace Christ brought us by His resurrection. To spread that Gospel today, as quickly as possible, is the only justification for our existence.

But more. It often takes courage to plant a church, to organize a congregation. Just so, we ought to be courageous enough to close up a church when the welfare of the Kingdom demands it. The needs of communities change from time to time. Where in days of yore two churches and two pastors were often needed to bring the bread of life to men, today, through changes brought about by time, one church and one pastor could supply those needs. But then we hear: How can you think of closing our church? Don't you know my grandfather donated that ground and that bell and that crucifix? — Close it, we say, if it stands in the way of opening the doors of heaven to those who know not the King! — To us the souls of men shall ever be more important than bricks and bells and benches. That, too, takes courage in the mission field, to know and act when a new piece of machinery is needed to do the King's work.

Furthermore. You are a young congregation. You possess only one small building. I know that you are thinking of the future in terms of new buildings, new school, new church, new parsonage, and the like. Those will be days of heavy debts. God help us in that day that it will be faith in action and not pride in action. That can happen. The peace of God which I bring you will be just as effective in this little chapel as in a quarter-million-dollar church edifice. In those days people usually begin to cut corners. I know which corners will be cut first — the dark corners of the world where Christ's peace has not yet been proclaimed. When under the stress of such a program the congregation cannot make ends meet, it makes possible the impossible by closing its eyes and ears to the crying needs of *the ends of the earth* to which the King has sent us. Too heavy a budget at home means too heavy a burden to bear for those abroad. If Easter and its peace mean anything to us then, no matter what our future program may call for, the ends of the earth shall hear from us the call to repentance, the call of the King to find peace in Him.

The peace we enjoy as subjects of the King we will ever be willing to share with all in our community. We will work zealously to bring the peace of God to them by our personal testimony. With our prayers and gifts we will support the representatives of the King on foreign soil. Our feet shall not rest until the world is resting in peace at the feet of the King.

IV. Peace Be unto You

Easter Sunday was drawing to a close. The two Emmaus disciples had brought the message to the Apostles in Jerusalem. But, Mark adds sorrowfully, *neither believed they them.*[23] While the two were still relating their experiences of the day, *Jesus Himself stood in the midst of them and saith unto them, Peace be unto you.* Now they saw, now they knew, now they believed, now they had peace — peace in all eternity.

From that day forward the world could no more impede the forward march of the King's army. Neither fire nor sword, neither gates of empire nor gates of hell could prevail against the onward rush of this new kingdom. The King of Peace calls men of peace to build His kingdom with weapons of peace.

You are the King's men. By His forgiving grace He brought peace to your heart. As you today stand at His altar to receive His body and blood in the Sacrament, He renews His bond of peace with you. In the power of that peace He sends you forth to bring peace to your home, peace to your nation, peace for all the world, and finally, for you, the peace of heaven.

Now, unto the King eternal, immortal, invisible, the only wise God, be honor and glory forever and ever.[24] . . .

> *In Thee all fullness dwelleth,*
> *All grace and pow'r divine;*
> *The glory that excelleth,*
> *O Son of God, is Thine.*
> *We worship Thee, we bless Thee,*
> *To Thee, O Christ, we sing;*
> *We praise Thee and confesss Thee,*
> *Our glorious Lord and King.*[25]

Amen

BIBLE REFERENCES

THE GLORY OF HIS PERSON

1. Acts 4:20
2. Ps. 24:8
3. Ps. 24:8
4. Ps. 24:9
5. Matt. 2:2
6. John 1:49
7. Luke 19:28
8. Is. 9:6
9. Jer. 23:5
10. Dan. 7:14
11. Col. 2:9
12. Luther
13. Nicene Creed
14. Matt. 21:9
15. Luke 2:14
16. Matt. 27:11
17. Matt. 27:29
18. John 19:15
19. John 19:15
20. Luke 23:38
21. Matt. 27:42
22. John 20:18
23. Acts 17:6f.
24. Is. 55:11
25. John 1:14
26. Matt. 7:14
27. Matt. 7:13
28. Gal. 3:27
29. Hymn 162, v. 1

THE GLORY OF HIS PURITY

1. Ps. 2:2
2. John 11:53
3. John 16:2
4. John 16:3
5. John 3:19
6. Hymn 657, v. 3
7. Luke 19:38
8. Luke 23:21
9. Luke 19:37
10. Matt. 21:10
11. Jer. 50:22, 26
12. John 1:29
13. Matt. 3:10
14. Matt. 3:12
15. Heb. 12:29
16. John 3:6
17. Gal. 4:4
18. John 3:6
19. Gen. 3:22
20. Jer. 23:6
21. Deut. 32:18
22. 1 Cor. 10:4
23. Deut. 32:32
24. Is. 5:2
25. Hos. 10:1
26. Luke 1:49
27. Luke 2:32
28. Acts 10:38
29. John 8:46
30. 1 Peter 2:22
31. Mark 1:24
32. John 8:33
33. Mark 10:4
34. Mark 7:11
35. Rom. 3:27
36. Rom. 3:9
37. Rom. 3:23
38. Is. 56:7
39. Prov. 20:8
40. 1 Cor. 3:16
41. 1 Tim. 5:22
42. Ps. 24:9
43. Rev. 3:20
44. Gen. 2:17
45. Jer. 30:17
46. Luke 6:19

THE GLORY OF HIS PRECEPTS

1. John 1:9
2. Matt. 21:22
3. Matt. 21:25
4. Matt. 21:27
5. John 12:21
6. Matt. 26:15
7. Rom. 13:10
8. John 17:8
9. John 13:34

10. 2 Cor. 3:6	16. 1 John 5:20	22. 1 John 4:7
11. Heb. 3:4	17. 1 John 4:19	23. Luther
12. Jer. 29:13	18. Luther	24. Matt. 5:44
13. James 2:19	19. Ps. 119:104, 97	25. Luther
14. Deut. 6:4	20. Deut. 10:19	
15. John 14:8	21. Luke 10:30	

THE GLORY OF HIS PROPHECIES

1. Matt. 21:34	12. Gen. 28:14	23. Matt. 24:3
2. Matt. 21:37	13. Hos. 13:9	24. Dan. 9:27;
3. Matt. 20:18	14. Luke 21:5f.	12:11
4. Matt. 20:19	15. Luke 21:20	25. Matt. 24:15
5. John 3:14	16. Luke 19:41-44	26. Matt. 24:29
6. John 13:11	17. Matt. 27:25	27. Rev. 22:12
7. Mark 8:31	18. Jer. 22:29	28. Luke 23:11
8. Phil. 2:9	19. Luke 21:27	29. John 12:26
9. Lev. 11:1	20. Matt. 26:64	30. Matt. 24:31
10. Gal. 3:24	21. Matt. 24:36	31. Phil. 1:6
11. Gal. 3:7	22. Rev. 16:15	

THE GLORY OF HIS PASSOVER

1. Ex. 11:5	10. John 13:20	18. John 17:22
2. Ex. 12:5	11. John 13:27	19. John 17:23
3. Ex. 12:7	12. John 13:33-38	20. John 17:24
4. Ex. 12:28	13. John 14:2-6	21. Hymn 310, v. 4
5. Ex. 12:13	14. John 14:8f.	22. 1 Cor. 10:16
6. Ex. 12:37	15. John 14:22-26	23. Matt. 9:2
7. John 1:29	16. John 16:33	24. Ps. 6:6
8. Luke 22:24	17. John 17:11	25. Is. 64:6
9. John 13:8		

THE GLORY OF HIS PRAYER

1. 1 Peter 3:18	8. Gal. 4:4	14. Heb. 4:15
2. Ex. 5:2-4	9. Phil. 2:7	15. 2 Cor. 12:9
3. Dan. 3:14f.	10. Dan. 5:1-4	16. Eph. 2:1
4. Matt. 17:5	11. Dan. 5:27	17. Matt. 18:14
5. John 10:32	12. Dan. 5:30	18. Is. 53:6
6. John 9:4	13. Hymn 154, v. 2	19. Hymn 400, v. 5
7. Heb. 9:20-22		

111

The Glory of His Priesthood

1. Hymn 159, v. 2
2. Matt. 26:31
3. John 18:14
4. Is. 53:7
5. John 1:11
6. Heb. 7:14
7. Heb. 7:23 f.
8. Heb. 5:5
9. Ps. 110:4
10. Heb. 7:26
11. Heb. 4:15
12. Heb. 2:17
13. Matt. 26:68
14. 1 Peter 2:9
15. Alfred Tennyson, "The Passing of Arthur"

The Glory of His Passion

1. 2 Tim. 4:2
2. Luke 23:33
3. Luke 23:46
4. Luke 23:38
5. Rom. 5:12
6. Job 30:23
7. 2 Sam. 14:14
8. John 10:10
9. Matt. 16:21-23
10. Gal. 4:4
11. Heb. 10: 4, 12, 14
12. Rom. 1:16
13. Mark 15:43
14. Matt. 19:24
15. Is. 55:1
16. John 3:3
17. Is. 55:11
18. Hymn 140, v. 3

The Glory of His Promises

1. Matt. 26:35
2. Matt. 6:25
3. Luke 18:31-33
4. Matt. 11:28
5. Is. 41:10
6. Ps. 103:4
7. Ps. 105:14
8. Is. 53:5
9. Matt. 27:63
10. John 3:16
11. John 7:51
12. Rom. 6:18

The Glory of His Peace

1. Rev. 19:16
2. Is. 63:1-3
3. Rev. 19:13
4. 1 Tim. 6:15
5. Is. 9:6
6. Mark 16:6 f.
7. John 20:9
8. John 20:13
9. John 20:15
10. John 20:18
11. Mark 16:10 f.
12. Matt. 28:9 f.
13. Luke 24:10 f.
14. Is. 50:6
15. Matt. 9:2
16. John 16:33
17. Matt. 14:27
18. Rom. 1:4
19. Rom. 4:25
20. Titus 3:5
21. Jer. 31:3
22. John 15:13
23. Mark 16:13
24. 1 Tim. 1:17
25. Hymn 352, v. 3